3.00

VATICAN DIARY 1965

DOUGLAS HORTON

Vatican Diary 1965

A PROTESTANT
OBSERVES THE FOURTH SESSION OF
VATICAN COUNCIL II

United Church Press
PHILADELPHIA — BOSTON

Library of Congress Catalog Card Number 64-23949

His Eminence
Albert Gregory Cardinal Meyer

When in my previous diaries I so frequently made mention of the name of Cardinal Meyer among the giants of the council, it was untinged with any apprehension that in this last diary I should be speaking of him as having lived and having done his work.

As may be read in my every reference to him, I contemplated him always with delight and admiration. My very first encounter with him suggested something of the quality of the man. I was coming through the court to the south of St. Peters after one of the first congregations of the first session when I was aware of a tall and broad-framed man advancing to shake my hand. "I'm Meyer of Chicago," he said, "and I hope we're treating you well." The observers were being well treated indeed, but of all the acts of hospitality I had enjoyed, innumerable as they were, none made me feel more surely at home than this. This second-mile courtesy, wholly beyond the border of obligation, probably had a deeper effect upon me than I realized at the time, for in the cardinal I came to see the spirit of the council: it became to me warm, friendly, and, under its formality, most human.

One of my meetings with the cardinal is not mentioned in the diaries I have published previously, since it took place between the first and second sessions, in Chicago. After we had both given our impressions of the council at a meeting at which a number of Protestant ministers of the Middle West were assembled, he led us in a series of intercessions which closed the Week of Prayer for Christian Unity. This at the time was unprecedented, revealing his courage; it was done so feelingly as to reveal his complete commitment to Jesus Christ; and it was altogether so effective that the walls of division between him

5

and his non-Roman fellow-worshipers seemed suddenly no more substantial than those of Jericho when the trumpets of the Lord had been blown.

Most of us who were at the council will remember the cardinal chiefly as we saw him in the crisis of the last days of session III, recorded on pages 177-78, 183-85, and 190-92 of my diary for 1964. At that time when leadership was called for, men turned to him naturally. He had the breadth of mind not only to command that situation but also to see it contextually in the life of the total church. His utterances on the floor of the basilica had again and again shown his familiarity with the church's history and his closeness to its essential spirit. He was a theologian in action. All that he and the others who repaired to his banner at that time were asking was that the council be allowed to express itself and not to have its procedure determined by a committee or committees it could not control. Though the Holy Father thought it best on that occasion not to put his weight on the side of insuring to the council its own right of self-expression, at the fourth session (as the reader of this diary will see), when a similar attempt was made to substitute committee control for the full suffrage of the council, His Holiness did support the council against the committee that wished to keep it mute—and on the same subject, religious liberty. This eventual acceptance of what the cardinal was requesting is in itself a tribute to his wisdom and foresight.

There is no need to list the other occasions at the council when the cardinal came to the fore. He was always at his post, listening to any who had anything to say, making his own contribution to the debate from his well-stocked mind, and in general laying his shoulder to the wheel and moving the whole church toward aggiornamento.

Now he has left us for the immortality God has granted him. Pray God that in our remembrance of him and in our faithful imitation of his strength and virtues we may give to him an immortality of influence in a world which he honored and blessed by his presence.

6

AUTHOR'S PREFACE

Partly as a penance for writing so voluminously and partly in order, in this last of my diaries, to correct such errors as may have crept into my previous narrative, I have read over what I have written about the earlier sessions.

I must apologize for any typographical mistakes that escaped my eye as I read proof. Errors of fact or impression, though none of them that I have discovered seem to be serious, also call for remedy. The Secretariat for Christian Unity, I think, had no direct hand in producing the texts on The Laity and the Church (1962, p. 176). I cannot believe that Cardinal Suenens is correctly quoted as speaking of *John*, rather than *Angelo Giuseppe*, Roncalli (1963, p. 99).

More interesting are discoveries I was not looking for, especially in the realm of change in my own attitudes. All of us observers were eventually drawn from the spectators' stand into the arena. We came to take sides on every issue. We approved this procedure, and disapproved that. And in this milieu I find myself at the end speaking less frequently and less enthusiastically about certain personalities than I did at the beginning—though I note on the other hand that many of those who early caught

the eye of my admiration emerged as heroic figures in my last
chapters.

Not only I but, more importantly, the council changed in the
course of the years. On October 18 in 1962, just as it was beginning, I sat in Fr. Stransky's apartment with a few Roman Catholic leaders who knew the church remarkably well (1962, pp.
32-33). They were unanimous in the thought that this council
could do little more than give the church a new orientation, and
that it would need a subsequent council, thirty to fifty years
hence, to make the *aggiornamento* that all desired. But what has
actually happened? The church has been largely freed from its
juridical scaffolding and is now ready to be the worshiping and
ministering company for which its Lord designed it. It has
sounded the note of religious liberty in every land. It has altered
its forms of worship in the direction of congregational participation. It has stretched out its hands in friendship to other
Christians and committed itself to the well-being of the world
in ways of which no previous council dreamed. The council not
only hit many of the marks it first aimed at but also lifted its
sights toward further goals. So far from merely updating its
forms and formulations, it has penetrated to new truth, not the
least of which is the apprehension that truth itself requires a
continuing will to discovery. The theological presuppositions of
"Congar and Rahner and Küng" (1963, p. 190), regarded as revolutionary at first, became, if not commonplace, at least widely
acceptable. The progressive majority, maintaining itself through
every vicissitude, proved itself a matrix for growth for the total
church.

If I had been able to look at the beginning from the point of
view of the end, I should have made much more of the proposal
of Cardinal Liénart (1962, pp. 22-23) that the council should not
accept, out of hand, the slate of commission members nomi-
nated by the powers-that-were at the time, but should rather
give itself a period to consider all possible candidates and select
the ablest. I did not know then of the feverish telephoning in
which the progressives immediately engaged, tapping the re-

sources of personnel in every nation until they had assembled a list of forward-looking men which easily won its way when presented to the council. Today it is as clear as noonday that this was a germinal act giving life to the council, without which the subsequent history of the church would in all probability have been a mere continuation of the past.

I am amused to read of the hope I shared with many at each session, that that session would be the last. (1962, p. 31: "We hear rumors that the council will last more than a year!") When one now looks back on the council, it does not seem to have outlasted its necessities, though undoubtedly its procedures might have been improved at points.

Some ideas took on strength in the course of the council. Ecumenicity, for instance, began as a mustard seed, and now behold: it is a tree giving shelter to all. Something similar could be said of the doctrine of the laity. And as for the teaching regarding the status of bishops, conceived as a tenuous hope in the minds of the imaginative in the first days of the council, it was finally given a secure basis not only in the chapter on collegiality in the Constitution on the Church, but in the institution of the Episcopal Synod, which seems destined for many a productive rendezvous with the future.

To the United Church Board for World Ministries, its Executive Vice President, Dr. Alford Carleton, and his aides. I owe a special debt, for they made available to me for the four years of the council the dictating machine that I used daily to report my impressions.

To Msgr. Wilfrid H. Paradis, who served as *peritus* to our Bishop Primeau of Manchester, New Hampshire, my fullest thanks go out again. There is surely no more certain token of Christian grace than the willingness to read another man's manuscript in advance of publication, but it is just that which Msgr. Paradis has done for me. I cannot hope that he has protected me from all the blunders into which my ardor may have led me, but I know that he has saved me from the direr ones.

I suppose that there are those who sigh for the golden yesterdays when, for all our wooden ships, we had our men of steel —and in the church, for all its relative weakness, our prophets of power. But I find myself doing nothing of the sort. I never had more confidence in the church than I have today, and that to no small extent because, for four years, I have sat as a listener at Vatican Council II.

DOUGLAS HORTON

Randolph, New Hampshire

CONTENTS

THE FIRST WEEK

📖 *Tuesday, September 14, 1965*

Here beginneth the Epistle from the Romans, the fourth chapter.

That the experience of the ecumenical council has been educational even for those who administer it was brought out clearly in the structure of the great opening service. It began on time, or almost on time. It lasted for only two and a half hours, a fitting length for even so solemn a celebration, and far more fitting than the five hours of the original opening service three years ago when, toward the end, solemnity shaded off into somnolence. This service had splendor without flamboyance. The council fathers were garmented in their striking crimson, but unmitred. The Pope himself, following the example of John XXIII on the first day, walked the whole length of the nave, and without the great nodding eastern fans that were wont to accompany him. Though the order of service called for his being borne out of the basilica in his *sedia gestatoria* on the broad shoulders of his carriers, even this was forgone. The lights that on previous occasions had given something of a Christmas-tree touch to the apse were not in evidence. There was no tinsel: every circumstance seemed to announce that the council was ready to get down to its momentous business.

Msgr. Davis, our trusted interpreter, whom I was delighted to
find sitting just behind me, spoke of having just read in his
breviary that on one occasion the Emperor Heraclius, expected
to carry a great cross in a procession, could not do so because he
was wearing so many vestments. Just as the emperor freed himself to carry his cross by divesting himself of excess in finery,
Pope and council members (who had of course read the same
passage in the breviary) now seemed to be freeing themselves
for the strenuous days ahead.

The opening mass was concelebrated at the high altar by the
Holy Father with twenty cardinals and six bishops and archbishops, who composed the council presidency, moderatorship, and
secretariat. It symbolized at once the council's unity and its dedi-
cation to Christ.

After the mass the Pope was escorted to his throne under the
baldachin, only to leave it almost immediately in order to place
on the altar at the head of the nave the copy of the Gospels, a
treasure among the manuscripts of the Vatican library, which,
opened to the first chapter of the Gospel According to John—
"In the beginning was the word"—has served from its high position on the altar as a symbol of the dominance of the gospel in
the debates of the council from their very beginning. Others have
been the Gospel-bearers, a different father each day, in the previous sessions: that the Pope himself should perform this act
was significant in itself.

In previous opening services a good deal of attention had been
paid (and a good deal of time given) to the "obediences" of
cardinals, patriarchs, archbishops, bishops, abbots, and superiors
general to the Pope. I still remember my first impression of the
tottering line of aged cardinals making their way to the papal
throne. But today this was all reduced to a token: two representatives from each group knelt before the Holy Father—another
tribute to organizational efficiency.

Presently came what all had been waiting for—the allocution
of the Pope. Just three days before, in an encyclical to be known
as *Mysterium fidei*, he had exhorted the Roman Catholic world

to follow the traditional interpretation of the Lord's Supper and condemned such theologizing about it as would disturb the faith of the faithful. Extreme critics had seen both in the content and timing of this document a papal declaration of war against too much *aggiornamento*. Those of my own turn of mind, although we felt that it was most legitimate for the Pope to express his own opinion on the matter, had prayed inwardly that the effect of it would not be to suppress the spirit of inquiry among Roman Catholics in eucharistic studies. Undoubtedly many at the council, remembering the encyclical, harbored the fear that the Pope's first utterance at this session would stamp him as a conservative desiring just as little updating as possible.

To the delight of the progressive forces, as the Pope was bringing his utterance to an end, he made an announcement which, so far from freezing the church into its present molds, may actually serve to guide it into a new era of strength and service. He announced his decision to establish a senate of bishops. This is to be called a synod "for consultation and collaboration." It will meet at the call of the Pope to assist him in the government of the church.

It has been well known that such a synod has been desired by a large majority of the bishops. Their votes have prepared the way for it. I have felt for a long time that it might be the keystone of the arch of *aggiornamento:* without it the church would tend to lapse back into the status quo, but with it, hopes would be bright for a church evolving into increasingly relevant ministries to the world. Actually I had feared that the recent additions to the college of cardinals meant that the Pope was planning to make that appointed body a kind of interim council of bishops; but now, for the first time in history so far as I know, authority is to be given to the various conferences of bishops throughout the world to appoint their own representatives to Rome to meet the Holy Father, advise and be advised by him, and in general provide a body of field generals to offer a creative balance to the curia of staff generals. It is hard to imagine anything more momentous in the long history of this church, which until now has been devoted almost wholly to the monarchical and nondemocratic idea. The Pope promised that he would soon fill in the outlines of his plan with needed details.

The bishops did not applaud this announcement, being perhaps too abashed at their own victory, but they clapped freely when the Pope went on to speak of his one-day visit to the United Nations in New York to plead for peace among the nations of men.

Applause also followed the announcement of the Secretary General that tomorrow the first subject for debate will be the *schema* on religious liberty. This means, once again, that the soothsayers of gloom, who have held that this document would never again see the light of day, have been wrong. Events, indeed, seem now to be moving so surely toward *aggiornamento* that one can almost understand why the truly conservative are frightened and why the Holy Father, in order to keep both conservatives and progressives within the loving embrace of the church, feels it necessary, now and then, to let the world know, as he did in reference to the Holy Eucharist, that the church is not abandoning its time-honored beliefs.

In the late afternoon the Pope led the council fathers in a penitential procession from the basilica of the Holy Cross of Jerusalem to that of St. John Lateran. This proved to be more of a penance for the bishops than they had anticipated, for they had to wait an hour before the procession began, had to walk the half mile, had to wait another hour before the beginning of the service that was to climax the event, had to listen to a very long sermon, and finally in order to get home had to make their way through an almost impenetrable crowd.

ᴆ *Wednesday, September 15, 1965*

The first general congregation of the fourth session and the 128th general congregation of the Second Ecumenical Vatican Council assembled this morning at 9:00 o'clock. As a matter of fact, it began before that, for while the council fathers were still chatting in the aisles, announcement was made that the Pope would not only attend the mass at the beginning but would also stay over for the first item of business.

Before the mass began, we were all given beautifully printed orders of service for the masses for the whole session. This marks an improvement over the masses of the previous session, for the new forms allow for considerably more congregational participation and provide grateful variety in place of the almost constantly repeated Mass of the Holy Spirit.

Another innovation will contribute to the time-saving program to which the organizers of this session are clearly committed. The Gospel will not be carried down the long nave to the singing of hymn or creed between mass and congregational meeting: it will now be enthroned on a lectern before the altar at the beginning of the mass, being brought in as part of the ceremony of entrance of the celebrant of the mass and his ministers.

The Holy Father was with us almost before we knew it, for he too entered by the shortest route, from the north transept just behind our tribune.

For the mass the Pope occupied a seat midway between the moderators and the altar at the head of the nave. The mass over, he was escorted to the central seat at the table of the presidents, in symbol of the fact that he is the head of the college of bishops.

Now the Secretary General made the announcement, breathtakingly close to the preliminary word of yesterday, that the Pope was present to hear the reading of the detailed plans he had established for the episcopal synod and to promulgate them as the law of the church forthwith.

Cardinal Marella, chairman of the council's Commission on Bishops and the Government of Dioceses, introduced the reading in a brief speech in which he referred to the time and thought that had gone into the plans for the synod—which should now be matched by the bishops themselves making ready for cooperation through their national and international conferences. I do not think that they will need much urging along this line.

As the Secretary General read the twelve articles of the new legislation, few could have failed to be aware that a new milestone was being set up on the church's road into the future. The introduction pointed to the meeting of the council as the occasion (though not the cause, since it was finally the Pope's doing) for establishing a permanent and representative council of bishops. And everyone present, I believe (because we think in wishes) found his mind running to the happy conclusion that this session of the council would now surely end before Christmas, since it could leave to the new synod the matter of crossing the t's and dotting the i's of its legislative documents. Though the function of the synod will be only to provide advice and counsel, it will enjoy such prestige that the advice and counsel will be reinforced by ample authority. Though it will be called together by the Pope, it will have a permanent secretariat. It will be composed of patriarchs, major archbishops and metropolitans, bishops chosen by the national conferences of bishops (who will constitute the bulk of the membership), bishops chosen by international conferences in which several nations participate, ten representatives of religious orders, and the cardinals in charge of various organs of the Roman curia. The Pope may add members, but never more than 15 percent of the total. It is wisely ordered that membership in any particular meeting of the senate expires at the completion of the senate's work: this means that there will be no feature of permanency to give the members the same complexion, and make them subject to the same distrust, as the members of the curia.

After saying the words that established the plan as law, the
Pope gave his blessing to the assembly and left the council hall,
not without what the newsmen later in the day called "an affectionate gesture" toward the observers. We joined in warm applause.

Cardinal Tisserant, senior president of the council, then read
a brief word of greeting—an *avete* to the fathers who were pres-
sent for the first time and a *valete* to those who had died since
the last session. He assured the fathers that there would be no
interference with freedom of speech—and if he will stand by this
promise, I am sure that all will forgive him his act of cloture
at the end of the last session. He asked all speakers to refrain
from useless repetition and from wandering from the point, and
all listeners to refrain from applause.

After Cardinal Agagianian, moderator for the day, had contributed his own greetings to all and sundry, Archbishop Felici
read to the assembly a telegram received from the Ecumenical
Patriarch of the Eastern Orthodox Churches, the man in Orthodoxy closest to being the opposite number of the Pope. His good
wishes for the success of the council were greeted by the fathers
with loud applause.

Now Bishop de Smedt introduced the *schema* on religious
liberty in the name of the Secretariat for Christian Unity, which
had written it. In the main he stressed the point that the *schema*
is designed to declare that no civil authority has the right to
ask a man to act against his conscience in matters of religion.
Apparently the chief conservative objection to the *schema* is
that it seems to give truth and error equal rights: this the bishop
denied. The *schema* asserts only, said the bishop, that it is not
for the state to determine what is truth and what is error.

Cardinals Spellman of New York and Frings of Cologne stood
strongly for the substance of the *schema*. Cardinal Spellman
called it a *must*.

Cardinals Ruffini of Palermo, Siri of Genoa, and de Arriba y
Castro of Tarragona in Spain now advanced from the negative
end of the lists to break a spear or two in opposition to the

schema. Cardinal Ruffini was not as out-and-out as usual but, with Augustine, he plainly thought that people ought not to be given "liberty to be lost." (According to this philosophy, neither church nor state should be quite so liberal as God.) If Cardinal Ruffini saw the *schema* as dark gray, Cardinal Siri saw it as almost black, and Cardinal de Arriba y Castro as completely stygian. The latter announced that only a Catholic has the right to preach the gospel and that proselytism should be outlawed in every Catholic country. He based his observations on the Spanish philosophy that the common good implies common unity. He felt that the solution of the problem should be left in the hands of the various national episcopal conferences with the approval of the Holy See—a suggestion obviously not without merit, if the council will not retreat from the fundamental principles of the *schema*.

Cardinal Urbani of Venice, in the name of thirty-two Italian bishops, Cardinal Cushing of Boston in Massachusetts, and Cardinal Alfrink of Utrecht spoke as strongly for the *schema* as the three preceding had spoken against it. This is the second time that Cardinal Cushing's ringing Bostonese has been heard on the same subject. All rights, said he, must be based on truth and human good. The truth of this *schema* is that the dignity of man establishes his right to act according to his conscience. The human good involved is that such action should be immune from the repressive force of the state. Everyone (especially those of us who know of his contributions to public life in his own archdiocese) was ready to believe him when in his tremendous voice he said, in the spirit of the apostle Paul, "I am not ashamed of the Gospel of Freedom."

☞ *Thursday, September 16, 1965*

As soon as the council was ready for business this morning, the Secretary General made the welcome announcement of the proposed agenda for this final session.

There are four *schemata* to be debated—"Religious Liberty" (now on the floor), "The Church in the Modern World" (the pièce de résistance of the session), "The Missionary Activity of the Church," and "The Ministry and Life of Priests."

Two documents have already been debated and are ready for the final voting process—the *schemata* on "Divine Revelation" and on "The Apostolate of the Laity."

And five have already received initial votes of approval and now await voting on the amendments—"The Bishops' Pastoral Office in the Church," "The Renovation of Life in the Religious Orders," "Christian Education," "Priestly Training," and "The Relationship of the Church to Non-Christian Religions," especially Judaism.

From this it may be guessed how long the council will last—and none of the council fathers are hesitating to guess. Since the voting is worked painlessly into the general fabric of the council, being undertaken while other things are going on, it is only the debates on the first four subjects that should consume time. If three weeks are allowed for establishing the church's relation to the world (a theme to which three centuries might be given), and one week for each of the others, the council would need only six weeks to complete its docket. This, however, obviously provides too short a time for the commissions (especially the commission on the "The Church and the World") to read through and make judgments upon the often prolix and always numerous amendments. The problem of the presidents will be how to find the maximum of time for the commissions with a minimum of material for the calendar of the council itself. Bishop Primeau of New Hampshire suggested to a few of us in conversation a few

weeks ago that after the council had discussed the church in its
relation to the world, it might wisely confine its activity to three
days a week, leaving the other days for the commissions to over-
take their work. Some plan of this sort seems imperative.

In his introductory statement this morning, the Secretary General observed that the fathers had been writing out their amendments for the Secretariat on paper of all shapes and sizes—and
qualities. In order to save trouble for future historians undertak-
ing the study of council documents, the council would now
supply specially prepared forms.

Yesterday the speeches were five to three in favor of the
declaration on religious liberty. Today it seemed to be about the
same—ten to seven. Objection seems to come almost wholly from
the Spanish-speaking fathers, and chiefly from Spain itself. Archbishop Morcillo Gonzalez of Madrid, one of the secretaries, put
their case strongly. Admitting that the state is incompetent to
make judgment in religious matters, he argued that the state
should listen to the church. To me his logic broke down on the
point that the state, in selecting a particular church to listen to,
is really making a religious judgment. Archbishop Morcillo Gonzalez is a man who should be honored for his progressive action
in abolishing all "class distinctions" in religious ceremonies taking
place in his archdiocese: beginning this year there will be no
"first-class weddings" as opposed to "second-class weddings," for
instance, because all ceremonies will be of a standard nature, no
matter how much the principals involved contribute to the church
—but he does not shake himself loose from the Spanish idea of
the "Catholic State." After his speech Cardinal Ruffini walked
all the way from the presidents' table to that of the secretaries
to congratulate him on his intervention.

Bishop Velasco, a Dominican from China, expressed himself
with not a little personal emotion. He felt that the majority in
the council and on the commission had ruthlessly extinguished
the ideas of the minority. That "glorious minority" had been told
that it did not understand the text—but if council fathers after
long years of study and experience cannot understand it, what

chance is there of its being understood by the body of the people? The buzz of private conversation in the council rose perceptibly while the bishop was speaking. My guess is that the number of those who favor the *schema* is even larger than that hinted by the proportion of favoring speeches.

No one could have given the *schema* more telling support than was provided in Cardinal Ritter's salute to it. Its presentation was for him an occasion of great joy. The work done by the Secretariat for Christian Unity in revising the text leaves nothing more to be desired but the final approval and promulgation of the document. Let us freely confess that in some Catholic countries non-Catholics have suffered: where these sufferings were due to the constitution of the church itself, they will now be ended. The whole world should rejoice with us.

Cardinal Slipyi of the Ukraine, in the name of a number of patriarchs, bishops, and others from his part of the world, praised the document and asked that it specifically call for freedom from the state for churches on the dark side of the iron curtain. He was listened to as a man must be who carries scars for the truth he advocates.

Archbishop Nicodemo of Bari, usually found in the ranks of the conservatives, declared the *schema* good and even necessary, but he hoped that readers would not translate the freedom vis-à-vis the state, advocated by it, into freedom vis-à-vis the church. He feared that it might lead to a claim of false liberty within the church. I agree with him in his anticipation, though I would not say I fear such an outcome nor would I call such liberty false.

Several advised omitting the paragraph that opens the door to an established religion within a state, on the ground either that it is too short and oversimplified for so complicated a subject or for the more substantial reason that established religion in the long run generally tends toward injustice at some point or other.

In the name of several of his fellow nationals, Archbishop Aramburu of the Argentine pointed to the unfortunate implica-

tions of the expression "public peace" as the reason for limiting
the exercise of religious liberty. He felt that the idea of justice
or natural law should be substituted for this so that civil authorities should not have ground for declaring the preaching of the
gospel, or even demonstrations in behalf of civil rights, to be
against the public peace—and therefore forbidden.

꜀꜀ *Friday, September 17, 1965*

This morning was celebrated the Mass of the Holy Spirit, one
of seven formularies approved for council use, and virtually the
only one used at previous sessions. These formularies open the
door happily to congregational participation in the chants, but
one has to confess that so far this has been ragged and weak.
We miss the faultlessly beautiful motets of the choir and wish
that room might be found both for them and for our own honest
but amateur endeavors.

Yesterday morning the *adsumus,* the remarkable prayer that
stems from the tenth century and that has been said daily at the
council until now, was omitted. (This is the one that begins,
"We are here, O Lord, in spite of our sins, but gathered in thy
name . . .")It was used again this morning, however, and I
suspect that yesterday it was simply overlooked in the midst of
the novelty of the new formularies.

One advantage of having the book of the Gospels brought in
before, and not after, the mass, is that it is now possible to put
it to actual use in the mass itself. After the minister assisting the
chief celebrant has read from it, he carries it to the celebrant,
who kisses it in the Catholic—perhaps I should say Mediterranean—manner.

For the promulgation of the announcement regarding the
synod of bishops, the Pope's throne had been carried down from

its high tribune to the center of the presidents' table on the lower dais, where it is flanked by the presidents' chairs, six on each side. It is noteworthy and, I suppose, symbolic, that they are leaving it there for these subsequent sessions. Your very eye now tells you that the Pope is the head of the college of bishops.

At the beginning of the business session, Archbishop Felici announced that on this very day Cardinal Maximos IV Saigh, Melchite Patriarch of Antioch, is celebrating the sixtieth anniversary of his ordination to the priesthood. The council broke into applause which, as the Secretary General remarked, was contrary to the rules, but according to the spirit, of the council.

From the count of the debaters on the two sides this morning —ten pro to eight contra—it might appear that the negative forces are gaining on the affirmative, but I do not think they are. From innumerable conversations with others, I judge that the forces of reaction are simply more vocal. In any case, these forces seem to have given up the attempt to outlaw the *schema* entirely and for the most part appear to be pushing toward a compromise. Their basic fear is that Catholic Christianity will lose its privileged position in theory and actuality. Arguing that religious truth as possessed by the Catholic is absolute and objective, whereas that possessed by others is simply subjective (the truth as they see it, merely), they do not like to have the doors of religious liberty opened equally to each. The problem becomes largely semantic, for most of these men argue for complete toleration of non-Christian faiths which are not antisocial. The two philosophies work out the same way today in practice. It is because it is felt, however, that the difference is not completely theoretical and that in another day it might show itself to have practical implications that the lines are definitely drawn and the emotions high on either side.

In a completely irrelevant parenthesis Cardinal Heenan, Archbishop of Westminster, praised the Pope's recent encyclical about eucharistic orthodoxy—so declaring himself theologically conservative—but the substance of his speech was an immensely strong defense of the *schema*. Mimeographed copies of his speech having been made available to observers, in its original English, I am able to quote verbatim: "It is quite absurd to talk of error not having rights—or, for that matter, of truth having rights. Rights are vested in people, not in things. It is the inviolable right of a man to obey his conscience provided he commits no breach of the peace and does not invade the rights of others." No one could have put the argument of the declaration more clearly.

Cardinal Conway, Archbishop of Armagh, added the note that it is against religious freedom for the state to make grants to schools with the provision that religious instruction be not given.

When Cardinal Ottaviani rose to speak, the assembly was hushed, not only because his Latin, like his thinking, is clear as a bell, but because it was thought that he might be speaking for the Holy Office itself, of which he is the chief. "The text gives equal value to both truth and falsehood: it reaches certain conclusions which are not to be commended but only to be tolerated because of the greater evil to be avoided." This seemed like something of a quiet retreat from his former intransigent position. The progressives, however, will not want to accept this compromise: for them religious liberty of all kinds is a human right, good in itself and not a lesser evil.

Archbishop Cantero Cuadrado of Sargossa, a member of the Secretariat that drafted the document, is the only Spanish speaker I have heard who seems to support the out-and-out kind of religious liberty the document sets forth. He had minor reservations, one of them deriving from the hope that the declaration would not provide a protection for conscientious objectors.

As usual, Archbishop Elchinger, Coadjutor of Strasbourg, brought fresh material to the debate. We should speak not only of the rights, but also of the duties, of conscience. No deep arguments for religious liberty should be delved for; the document should portray the church as the *obvious* protector of all transcendental human values: it is concerned for anything that is for the good of man's soul, like the spirit of inquiry. Our declaration should be a brotherly invitation to cooperation to all men of goodwill.

Bishop del Campo y de la Bárcena of Calahorra balanced the rights of man against the rights of God, and found the former relatively weak. And then, equating the rights of God with those of the church, he found in the declaration a contradiction of the right of the church to preach throughout the entire world. This voice of old Spain was countered by that of Bishop Rupp of Monaco, who read to the assembly the seven statements on religious liberty recently voted by the World Council of Churches in Geneva, and affirmed them all. He thought the present *schema* too discursive.

Bishop Maloney, Auxiliary of Louisville, made a telling point. He cited the fact that right here in St. Peters many contradictory statements had been made, some of which must obviously be erroneous. Whence comes the right to make such erroneous statements? Certainly it is not from any special privilege enjoyed by truth, since they are not true. Liberty of speech here is the personal right of each council father. It is this that the church should strive to impart to the whole world. Archbishop Hallinan of Atlanta also lauded the document: by assenting to religious liberty, the state is simply asserting its own limitations.

Our weekly meeting with the Secretariat for Promoting Christian Unity, usually held on Tuesday afternoons, took place this afternoon, since Tuesday was occupied with the little matter of opening the council. Bishop Willebrands presided.

Fr. John Courtney Murray introduced the *schema* on religious liberty in a way that revealed his knowledge not only of the document itself but also of the whole area of Christian ethics in which the subject of religious liberty lies. In answer to certain critics he pointed out that the document is based not on the passing social situation of today but upon the eternal truth of the dignity of the human person. He hoped the *schema* would open the way to full dialogue with the World Council of Churches and men of goodwill everywhere. As late as the nineteenth century the church regarded the state as being, as it were, within it, part of itself. Then came the great revolutions, which the church did not understand. Only today the church is coming to see the state as secular, but in a good sense—not hostile or indifferent to religion, but concerned only for the good of the human person, justice, charity, and freedom.

In the course of the discussion it became evident that most of the suggestions made by the observers had already been considered by the Secretariat during the now long period of gestation of the *schema*.

Dr. Canavatis, legal counselor of the patriarchal throne of Alexandria, felt that the *schema* needed the reinforcement of a strong theology based on the doctrine of the Holy Spirit. Bishop Willebrands pointed out that a long preparatory statement on the theology of freedom had been prepared but that it had been omitted for brevity's sake. Fr. Murray spoke of the need for theological studies connecting Pauline freedom with the modern conception.

Archimandrite Scrima, personal representative of the Ecumenical Patriarch in Istanbul, also made a comment characteristic of Orthodoxy. Instead of stressing "natural reason," he would like to see the *schema* bring out the spiritual values of liberty in the history of salvation. He felt that the church idea of liberty, expressed in the drama of the liturgy, would be a welcome substitute for the Western idea of liberty based upon simple individualism. Fr. Murray suggested that if the speaker would look below the arid surface style of the document, he would find the values for which he was asking.

The first two speakers among the observers were a reminder that, though Orthodoxy as a whole has sent no delegates to the council, being impeded chiefly by the negative vote of the great Church of Greece, the titular head of Orthodoxy is personally represented by Archimandrite Scrima and others; and besides this, four churches within Orthodoxy have now sent delegates in full standing—the Patriarchate of Alexandria three, the Church of Russia three, the Church of Bulgaria one, and the Church of Georgia one.

Professor Subilia of the Waldensian Theological Seminary in
Rome now asked if it would not have been better to begin the
schema with Christology instead of the philosophical appeal to
human dignity. He also felt it dangerous to suggest the possibility
of the establishment of any one religion in a state. In response
to the latter, Professor Murray hinted that the paragraph in question in the *schema* might be altered or even removed.

Professor Cullmann of the Universities of Basel and Paris
praised the document warmly, calling it a great improvement
over the edition of two years ago—"a truly historical event"—
but suggesting (doughty Protestant that he is) that it might be
given a more biblical basis. He made the interesting contribution
that the matter of recognizing the rights of the erroneous conscience might be supported by a reference to the apostle Paul's
attitude toward the eating of meat offered to idols. (I am not
sure, however, whether this would lead to freedom for non-
Christian faiths or only to tolerance.) Bishop Willebrands indicated that innumerable conferences had been held with biblical
experts on this and all other matters in the *schema*.

Pastor Roux of Paris, a former observer now making a return
visit, hoped that the final text would bring out, beyond a perad-
venture, that Christian faith itself involves respect for human
dignity. Fr. Murray supported the point by pointing to Christ's
refusal to establish his kingdom by force—a reference that had
indeed been written into an earlier text.

Anent the desire of Bishop Sarkissian, dean of the Armenian
Theological Seminary in Lebanon, that the *schema* should pro-
nounce proselytism an evil practice, Fr. Murray showed that
though the word proselytism had not been used in the text, the
thing itself had been described there. This device lessened the
threat the "sleeping hound to wake."

Professor van Holk, who has long kept the Remonstrant flag
flying at the University of Leiden, saved us from wandering too
far into stuffy theologistics (an extremity to which even biblical
theology may succumb) by the very tone of his remarks. He
asked that the document speak with unmistakable clarity against

the misuse by the state, in dealing with minorities, of the argument from "public interest." He also spoke as a modern man against conceiving truth and error as static and independent rather than as dynamic and developing entities in dialectic with each other. I thought of the Latin saying *Virescit vulnere virtus* and the schoolboy howler which translated it "Virtue is vulnerable but when vulned, she is always invigored." Truth is indeed vulnerable to error, but its tension with error keeps it strong and alive. Fr. Murray agreed with Dr. van Holk, and Bishop Willebrands observed that many bishops are not really in touch with the thought that enriches the life of today, makes it different from yesterday, and gives it great promise.

Dean Root of Emmanuel College in Cambridge, England, expressed the hope that someone would respond to the crystal-clear comments of Cardinal Ottaviani with equally clean-cut candor. Fr. Murray agreed, but pointed out the evolution in the cardinal's thought: whereas two years ago he had assumed that the church's attitude on religious liberty was a closed question, he was now willing to call it "controverted." He Christianly called the cardinal's the "classical" Catholic mentality. I have heard other descriptions of it.

☞ *Saturday, September 18, 1965*

This afternoon Cardinal Bea gave a reception to the observers. In the course of his formal speech to us, characteristically gracious, he mentioned that the number of observers has now grown to 99—over against the 49 of the first session—and that there are now 28 churches represented among them, instead of 23. Being asked by our steering committee to do so, I responded briefly to the cardinal in remarks that took the shape of a brief tribute to him, a man whom we have come greatly to admire.*

---

* See Appendix III of this diary.

📖 *Sunday, September 19, 1965*

Today Mildred and I worshiped at the local Methodist church, hearing a sermon by Dean Cannon of the Candler School of Theology, Emory University, Atlanta, Georgia, on religious liberty, the theme that is exercising the consciences of the council fathers.

THE SECOND WEEK
[SEPTEMBER 20-26]

📖 *Monday, September 20, 1965*

Yesterday after church Al Outler told us that he had heard that the *schema* on religious liberty was in trouble and that the presidents of the council, in response to a petition by over a hundred bishops, had decided to postpone the voting upon it—and this morning the newspapers seemed to support this doleful prognostication. This would mean that the delaying tactics of the last two years would again be applied, and possibly again succeed. So today we waited with bated breath for an undesired announcement.

But no such announcement came.

The debate went on, and is likely to be carried on for a day or two more; and in view of the tenseness of emotions it is surely the part of a wise moderatorship to allow the minority to have its say to the last man. As the day has advanced, indeed, I have grown more and more skeptical about the truth of the rumor. Direct word from one *peritus* who occupies a high seat indicates that the presidents have not acceded to the request of the conservatives, and indirect word from another discloses that the form of the vote on religious liberty is already being considered—which would hardly be the case if there were to be no vote. So I think the ship is still on course in spite of inclement seas—or perhaps I should say sees.

33

Before the business meeting began this morning, the Secretary General read a letter prepared in behalf of the council to be sent to the Holy Father. It expressed warm thanks to His Holiness for establishing the synod of bishops. "It now becomes our concern to obey and cooperate." It also thanked the Pope for his encyclical on the Eucharist, promised prayers for the success of his prospective trip to New York, and asked his blessing. The clapping hands of the fathers signified their approval. An account of the felicities of Felici should not omit his appeal to the fathers who had forgotten to bring with them the text of the *schema* on divine revelation. Said the Secretary General, "Unfortunately there are no more available, so borrow a copy if you can—or at least get hold of one in the most honest manner possible."

The array of speakers for the affirmative this morning made it clear that the forces of progress are not lacking either in men or materiel. Of the nine cardinals who made their witness, only one was shadowed by negativism—Cardinal Browne of the Roman curia. Out of the caves of the past he drew the troglodyte theology that in a Catholic state the spreading of another religion is a violation of public morality.

In what contrast were the others! I cite, for instance, the Archbishop of Baltimore, who made his maiden speech as a cardinal. In a historical address which showed in a most satisfying way the steady evolution of the definition of religious freedom in the church from the time of Leo XIII to the present day, he cannot but have been convincing to the more thoughtful of the fathers.

Cardinal Beran, Archbishop of Prague, who had just stepped out of prison, to which his championing of religious freedom had condemned him, needed hardly to say a word to be convincing. The marks and memories of his incarceration were his eloquence. The council cannot have been impervious to his plea to approve the document as it stands, without dilution.

Equally telling was the testimony of Cardinal Cardijn—who had recently been elevated to his high office from the ranks of the priesthood, without ever having been a bishop, this because of his surpassing saintliness and his founding and developing of the worldwide organization of Young Christian Workers. His sixty years of experience with youth spoke for him when he said, "If this *schema* is not approved, the hope of tomorrow will be destroyed."

Of the four bishops who spoke this morning, only one condemned the declaration. Two Lefebvres were participants in the debate. The one, the cardinal, the Archbishop of Bourges, had spoken with complete clarity in meeting the several major objections of the conservatives, but now Archbishop Marcel Lefebvre proved himself a cousin so distant as hardly to belong to the same family. He argued that the *schema* really came from the pens of such eighteenth-century philosophers as Hobbes, Locke, and Rousseau and that it paid more attention to the human conscience than it did to the church. He wanted none of it. He is the Superior General of the Congregation of the Holy Spirit; one of my neighbor observers, in a not exactly neutral frame of mind, expressed the wish that the Holy Spirit might be admitted to the order.

Rome must surely see that Rome will be the chief sufferer if the declaration on religious liberty is finally defeated. The cock has crowed twice—in the second and third sessions. I remember Papini's description of Peter after the cock crew for the last time: "Then in the dim light of dawn the last stars saw a man staggering along like a drunkard, his head hidden in his cloak, his shoulders shaken by the sobs of a despairing lament." I do not think that Peter will take that course again today.

         Tuesday, September 21, 1965

This was a big day.
The mass this morning was sung throughout. I was pleased

to see that the leader was Fr. Heiser, Superior General of the Franciscans, whom we had first met in the crypt of the great Franciscan monastery at Assisi two years ago. The congregational singing of responses still gets A for effort but T (terrible) for performance, except in the case of those melodies that are so simple that they can be picked up even by the tone-deaf after two or three repetitions.

Oscar Cullmann fainted as he was entering St. Peters this morning, but we have learned this afternoon that his condition is not serious.

Before business began, the Secretary General announced that the Holy Father had decided to take with him to the meeting of the United Nations in New York a representation from the council itself. This is to consist of Cardinals Cicognani, Secretary of State; Tisserant, dean of the College of Cardinals; Agagianian, head of the Congregation for the Propagation of the Faith; Gilroy, Archbishop of Sydney, Australia; Spellman, Archbishop of New York, who will be the Pope's host while there; Caggiano, Archbishop of Buenos Aires, Argentina; Doi, Archbishop of Tokyo, Japan; and Rugambwa, Archbishop of Bukoba, Tanzania, Africa. It will be noted that they represent eight different corners of the earth. Applause greeted the secretary's suggestion that the Holy Father be thanked for this gesture.

No one, I am sure, could have failed to notice the absence of the senior presidents, the presiding moderator, and the Secretary General, from the mass. We pictured them attending some Star Chamber court where the fate of the *schema* on religious liberty was being decided. This proved to be not the truth, but the first cousin to it.

The morning started out like any other. A list of speakers was presented which was so long that it was clear that the last name would not be reached until tomorrow at least. That was not disturbing, however, for we noted on the list the name of many a Valiant-for-Truth, who would say a persuasive word—including Bishop Primeau of Manchester, New Hampshire. And the second cardinal to speak (after the conservative Dante) was a theologian of greatest weight, Journet, who put all of it behind his thorough-going approval of the *schema*. (He had been elevated to the cardinalate direct from his professorship at Fribourg because of his theological achievements, without having been a bishop.) The debate was continued by two other speakers, one on each side of the fence.

Then came the first intimation that this was to be a day of destiny: the council was told that the presidents considered that the debate had now run its course and was ready to be closed—and cloture was voted by a very large majority, standing. I thought it a bit odd at the time that all twelve presidents voted with the majority, though some of them, like Cardinal Ruffini, had not been distinguished for their advocacy of religious freedom.

Bishop de Smedt of the Secretariat for Christian Unity, who has often shown himself to be a polished orator, now proved himself a politic one as well. He thanked the fathers for their "very constructive criticism," named one by one the major objections that had been raised against the text, and in the name of the Secretariat promised that there would now be a third edition susceptible of winning unanimous approval. Applause.

On the heels of this speech, in the midst of a silence which filled the basilica, the Secretary General asked the fathers to vote on the following question: "Is the text on religious liberty, which is to be further altered in the light of Catholic teaching on the true religion and of the amendments proposed by the fathers in discussion and then submitted for approval according to the rules of the council, acceptable as a basis for a definitive declaration?"

This was the form of the vote decided upon by the procedural authorities. Usually such a vote asked simply: "Is the proposed text acceptable as a basis for a statement by the council?" The additions here were of course designed to meet the demands of those who feared that religious liberty would compromise the Roman Catholic Church's claim to uniqueness.

Even in its softened form the vote did not carry an assured

outcome. The strategy of the conservative forces had been postponement; and during the postponement they had built up the
belief that there was a very considerable negative minority, a
belief to which they themselves had become sincerely attached
and which they had communicated to others. Msgr. Davis reported that some of the men at the English college feared that
there might be as many as a thousand now opposed to the declaration. Al Outler wagered with me that there would be 350
negative votes, my bet being 450. All were agog to know how
the vote would come out. In an entirely unprecedented fashion,
the council simply waited for the first five or ten minutes of the
counting of the ballots. Nothing else was done. Nobody was in
the bars. None of the fathers were wandering about.

Presently the moderators decided that it would be as well to
introduce the *schema* on "The Church in the Modern World,"
and that was done. The *relatio* or presentation was made by
Archbishop Garrone of Toulouse, in the absence of Bishop Guano
of Leghorn, who was ill. He indicated that the commission had
stretched every nerve to have this long and complicated text
ready for the council and to include in it all of the suggestions
made by the fathers at the previous session. It is now divided
into two main parts, the former of which tries, in terms of general
principle, to repeat what the spirit is saying to the church on
the condition of man and whence man's salvation must come.
It goes into detail in describing human society today. It raises the
questions that are on the mind of the church, and it outlines the
answers that the church, as the people of God, is trying to give.
The second part refers more to specific problems of society. All in
all, an attempt is made to keep in mind the pastoral purposes of
the council and not to allow the text to become too abstract and
theoretical.

Before the announcement of the vote on religious liberty, which
all were awaiting, there was time for two to comment on the new
schema—Cardinals Spellman and Landázuri Ricketts, one of New
York, the other of Lima. Both thought that the new edition was a
great advance over the previous one and that with sundry

changes in content and style it would at least provide a good basis for future dialogue.

Now came the announcement of the critical vote. 1,974 to only 224 against! This is a vote of infinite consequence, because it not only establishes the promulgation of the declaration on religious liberty but also shrinks our idea of the strength of the opposition to the proportions of reality and eliminates it as a threat to the future. One of the arguments for postponement had been that it would cast a shadow on the Pope's influence at the United Nations if it were known that, as suspected, almost half the council opposed his *aggiornamento*. And now it is known that the opposition is only one in ten! The dragon was made of paper. And I owe a drink to Al Outler.

After the vote, time was left for only three more speeches on the subject of the church in the modern world. It is evident that emotions are not going to run high on this one, but it is equally clear that the council hardly knows what to do with it, since it is so long and so full of material. Cardinal Bea, the last speaker of the morning, made the most incisive criticism. He likes the document as a whole, but hopes that the many repetitions may be eliminated, that its subjects may be much more precisely defined, that the whole text will be reviewed in the light of the Scriptures, and above all, that the Latin will be improved. The Latin is unclear because, in many cases, classical words have been used for modern inventions.

While the fathers were moving out of the hall, after the final benediction, the word ran from lip to lip like wildfire and it is now an open secret that the happy denouement of the morning was due to the Pope's intervention. The Committee of Twenty-Six, which is the final authority for council procedure and which consists of the presidents, moderators, general secretariat, and chairmen of commissions, had met and voted by a small majority to postpone the vote on religious liberty! The argument about blunting the Pope's influence at the United Nations, which I have cited, apparently prevailed; and the rumor of yesterday was not without foundation. This morning, therefore, Cardinal Bea and

Bishop Willebrands (and perhaps others) had waited upon the
Holy Father to let him see that nothing could be more disgrace-
ful for the church than to represent to the world that it was hesi-
tant on the matter of religious liberty. And then had come the
telephone call from the papal apartment to St. Peters which had
saved the day. In a system in which a majority among twenty-
six men can thwart the will of two thousand, the balancing mech-
anism whereby the will of one endowed with due authority can
thwart that of so small a majority, can be counted something of
a blessing on occasion.

The Pope's intervention gives further ground for congratulation. He has been fortunately forced to break his informal pledge
not to intervene in council procedure. As I have previously observed, I believe strongly that he should not intervene as Pon-
tifex Maximus, but he is more than that; he is also the head of the
college of bishops, and as such I believe that he should not
hesitate to take any action which makes it possible for that college to express its will in council. The Pope has taken a long step
in the direction of fulfilling his role in collegiality.

This afternoon many of us observers went without siesta in
order to attend a meeting of the group to (a) vote to continue the
executive committee which had been in charge on our behalf for
four years, (b) appoint one of our number (Lukas Vischer) to
assist the Secretariat in setting up the Tuesday meetings, (c) arrange for our biweekly prayer services in the Methodist Church,
and (d) take up any other matters of concern to all. Under the
last heading it was left to the language groups to arrange for
such meetings as they wished, and Fr. Tom Stransky and I were
able to announce later that the first meeting of the English-
speaking contingent would be held on Friday afternoon of this
week. Dr. Boegner expressed the hope that the observers would
be able to move the authorities toward a liberalization of the
rules about mixed marriages, and though we turned the matter
over to the executive committee for investigation, it was the general feeling today, as it had been last year, that the observers
should not under any circumstances take on the semblance of a

pressure group.* I suggested the preparation of a statement of thanks to the council to be read at one of the morning congregations toward the end of the session, and George Williams broached the idea of our making a gift to the Pope or the council which would represent our gratitude in permanent and substantial form. These last two matters were also turned over to the executive committee.

From this meeting we went into our regular weekly conference with the Secretariat. As further evidence of the meaning of these conferences to the council, George Williams passed on to me a bit of information which he had had from Bishop Wright: ideas brought up at the conferences, when deemed worthy of consideration by the council itself, are sent on to the proper commissions by number, whether they come from members of the Secretariat or the observers. They are not identified by the name of the author, and the commissions, though they may make further inquiry if they wish to, normally let the ideas speak for themselves, whether they come from Catholic or non-Catholic sources.

Presiding at our meeting today was Bishop Willebrands, who introduced Msgr. Peter Haubtmann of Paris to conduct our discussion on the *schema* "The Church in the Modern World." He is the *peritus* who has been in the thick of the preparation of the text and who addressed us last year with such brilliance. In my diary of last year I made him "Canon Haubtmann" but this was an error in canonization. Perhaps it is prophetic: he is a man of great intellectual penetration.

Msgr. Haubtmann outlined the *schema* for us, dwelling a bit on the vicissitudes it had encountered in its progress through a long series of committee meetings. The commission had attempted to keep it in the evangelical rather than the legal mode; they had attempted to speak briefly of the opportunities of the

---

* Subsequently it was decided that those interested in the question should prepare a statement for the Secretariat and sign it as individuals, not as representatives either of their churches or of the body of observers as such. A copy of the document submitted will be found as Appendix II of this diary.

man reborn in Christ, but without neglecting the point of view of the unregenerate; they had tried to let the light of the eschatological future shine on the present, though perhaps without success; they felt (or he did, at least) that they might have sounded the ecumenical note more strongly; and they had all agreed that the heart of it was to give an accurate description of the mission of the church. Concrete methods of working out the church's purpose may be left to the various executive arms of the church to develop and put into practice.

When the time for comments came, Dr. Selassie, professor of the Ethiopian Orthodox Church at the University College of Addis Ababa, expressed disappointment that so little had been said about the social influence of the liturgy, and also hinted that the status of women was now so far advanced that it might have been proper to speak less of the equality between men and women and more of the necessity for racial equality. Msgr. Haubtmann indicated that the majority of his commission had shied away from the liturgical reference; and he thought the speaker a trifle optimistic about the status of women.

Fr. Emilianos, representative of the Orthodox Ecumenical Patriarch at Geneva, felt too wide a separation in the text between the church and the world. Msgr. Haubtmann, though agreeing that perhaps the work of Christ in the world outside the church was not sufficiently brought out, supported the distinction between church and world since it is clear that there is a part of the world which is not in the church.

Dr. Reid, Presbyterian, professor of dogmatics at the University of Aberdeen, Scotland, felt that the text, in its neglect of the spiritual dimension of the church, left the impression of the church as a kind of Red Cross organization. He also felt a weakness in the *schema* in its description of the "autonomy" of the world. For him, as for Bonhoeffer and other contemporary thinkers, "autonomy" meant that the world had come of age and, in a sense, was capable of responding to God's will without the mediation of the church. Msgr. Haubtmann pointed to passages in the *schema* which supported Professor Reid in this emphasis, but also mentioned the difficulty they had encountered in finding lay language to express the truth at this point—and he asked for suggestions. Bishop Willebrands thought that there was a parting of the roads for Catholic and Protestant thinking on this issue.

Fr. Scrima picked up and amplified the theme of Professor Selassie. Though not sympathetic with the idea of delay, he felt that the text could do with a little more maturing, especially in the area of the relation of worship to the world. He wished to see a heavier underlining of the sense of mystery in the church, and through the church, in the world. He wanted a "theandric" vision of the church as God at work in the world. To save the *schema* from being moralistic, he asked for less Western conceptualism and more stress on communion with God creating the cosmos today. Msgr. Haubtmann was in general agreement. Bishop Willebrands added that men do live by philosophies not of Christian origin—an area not looked at in the *schema*. Msgr. Haubtmann agreed here, too, again pointing to the difficulty of finding the proper approach to the commission.

Mr. Keighley of the local Methodist Church felt that the questions asked in the *schema* were as strong as the answers to them were weak. He thought that more attention should be given to the extension of sin in the world and its enormous interpenetration with the good. Msgr. Haubtmann agreed personally that everywhere ambivalence between good and evil is in evidence. He did not want to canonize human good: Christianity is a *struggle*. Here again he asked for suggestions to carry to his commission.

Anent the comment of Dr. Vischer of the World Council of Churches that cooperation between Catholic and non-Catholic Christians should be more heavily underscored in the document, and that consultations should be recommended also, Msgr. Haubtmann observed that he wished his commission would agree. Bishop Willebrands thought this an important point, since the divisions within Christendom obviously weaken the church's work in the world.

Professor Evdokimov of the Orthodox Theological Institute of

St. Serge in Paris, thought that a number of images employed
in the text—such as angels and demons—had lost their meaning
for modern man. Msgr. Haubtmann felt that at this point it was
best to stick to scriptural language, since images awaken such
different connotations in the various parts of the world. He
thought it most important that we all come to agreement as to
the meaning of the image of the "new man."

Fr. Thyssen of the Secretariat asked that the ecumenical spirit
be allowed to pervade the whole text. Msgr. Haubtmann regarded this as an achievement to be hoped for after the council.
Fr. Thyssen wanted it put into the text here and now, in general and in particular. Msgr. Haubtmann agreed but hinted that
he was not the only member of his commission. Bishop Willebrands concluded the discussion by expressing the hope (for us
all) that Msgr. Haubtmann would succeed in converting his entire commission to his point of view.

So the day is over. As I look back upon it, I see it as one of the
great moments of the council. Consider that one hundred years
ago in the eightieth article of the Syllabus of Pope Pius IX, the
Roman church declared, "If anyone says that the Pope can and
should be reconciled and make terms with progress, with liber-
alism and modernist civilization, let him be anathema." Today
that same church, through this council, has opened the way for
a declaration which begins, "In this present age there is an increasing awareness among men of the dignity of the human
person. This dignity demands that man in his activity may enjoy his own judgment and freedom, so that he is impelled not
by coercion but by the consciousness of his own duties. This
demand for freedom in human society should be applied most
particularly to religious matters. The church, attentively considering these human longings, intends to show how much they are
in agreement with truth and justice."

This giant called Rome, who has so long been asleep in the
arms of the lady Traditio, is beginning to open his eyes.

◷ *Wednesday, September 22, 1965*

Before the debate opened this morning, the Secretary General expressed congratulations to Cardinal Cicognani, Secretary of State, who tomorrow will observe the sixtieth anniversary of his ordination as priest—and celebrate mass here. The secretary was seconded by prolonged applause from the fathers.

Since Monday, the council has been interlarding its debates with balloting on the *schema* on divine revelation. The whole of it has been read in small portions, the last of them today, and on none of them has the negative vote been of consequential size. Even the vote of "approval with reservations," which is negative in immediate effect, has never risen above 313. Nothing could reveal more clearly than this the intellectual development of the council itself: at the first session there was a stout 40 percent minority voting against *aggiornamento* in this field. Today only 14 percent refused the declaration of the majority, and most of them simply had reservations about it.

Discussion on religious liberty was not quite ended with the vote of yesterday. This morning it was continued by four speakers, each of whom had secured the backing of seventy others—which is the price for permission to participate in this kind of aftermath. Few new ideas were offered, but worth recording are the last words of the last speaker, Bishop Ancel, Auxiliary of Lyons: "Since man must seek truth in a human manner and as God wishes, this obligation demands religious liberty."

It is interesting to see how the minority are taking the tidal wave which engulfed them yesterday. Before the vote, Archbishop Staffa, who is regarded as the chief architect of the successful plan to shelve the vote on religious liberty at the last session was seen during the coffee hour moving from group to group in an expansive mood obviously seeking to increase his forces by the method known in the States as "glad-handing." After the vote, one observer remarked that he looked "as small as

the little end of nothing whittled down"—but this was only his
own impression. To most of us the archbishop still seemed his
handsome and commanding self. And among his followers this
morning one felt a certain resilience. Bishop Grotti of Brazil
spoke for them when he said (just before the debate was closed
by Bishop Ancel): "We must not exaggerate the importance of
yesterday's vote, and we must see to it that the promises made
by Bishop de Smedt are faithfully kept." These were the promises to make the *schema* conform to true Catholic doctrine.

We have learned more about what went on behind the scenes
preliminary to the vote. It seems that the question of the vote
went to the Committee of Twenty-Six because the moderators
could not agree—Cardinals Döpfner, Lercaro, and Suenens strongly recommending the vote but Cardinal Agagianian holding out
against it with the idea of delaying the vote until it had gone
into the limbo of forgotten things. Bishop Carlo Colombo is more
and more named as an influential and catalytic personality in the
high circles of the church. As the "Pope's theologian" he is said
to have furnished the arguments for the Pope's intervention. In
fact, some say that the Holy Father is today under the inspiration of the Holy Spirit—in the shape of Bishop C. However they
are identified, we must all be grateful to the Pope and his advisers.

Now was resumed the verbose discussion on "The Church in
the Modern World." Almost all of the speakers took the yes-but
attitude. The *schema* throws abundant light on the problems of
our age, its aim is excellent, it is a vast improvement over the
previous edition, the commission deserves our gratitude, BUT
. . . and then would follow the adverse criticisms, which I can
only list:

The style is too diffuse.

The Latin leaves much to be desired.

The natural order of things is unfortunately confused with the
supernatural order.

The contribution of the church to the world is passed over in silence. (Said Cardinal Ruffini, "It is almost as if the council were getting down on its knees in shame.")

Too little is made of the supernatural mission of the church.

The solutions suggested for today's problems are only transitory.

Not enough attention is paid to the problem of the unbeliever.

Please do not drag out the debate on birth control any longer!

A wedge is driven in between the church at work and the church at prayer.

Something more adequate should be said about leisure time.

And about illness.

And architecture.

The *schema* abandons the scholastic method of thought.

It follows the scholastic method of thought too slavishly.

So it went. As I sat listening, I felt something like the man in the old tale who on coming to a stream and wanting to cross it, took his seat on the bank waiting till all the water should flow away. The debaters of this *schema* have, after all, all the world from which to draw their material, and the world is not running short of problems with which to supply them.

As a matter of fact, the handling of the *schema* of eighty-four pages at this stage of the council constitutes a procedural problem of vast dimensions. After the council is through with it, it must go back to the anvil of the commission, and the fires of the commission's forge, if the *schema* is to be hammered into shape, must be kept burning for weeks. Either a holiday is indicated for the midpoint of this session—a possibility which the fathers from far countries can hardly welcome—or the council must vote to leave the finishing touches to the synod of bishops, which will have fewer numbers but more time. Actually, it might not be bad strategy for the council to provide items for the agenda of the synod: these might serve not only for continuity but as a launching force.

This morning the mass was celebrated by Cardinal Cicognani, Secretary of State to His Holiness. The choir of St. Peters with its lovely motets was with us again for the first time this year. Apparently the affairs of state have not closed the Cicognanian ears to music.

The voting on the *schema* on divine revelation having been disposed of, that on the apostolate of the laity was now introduced by Bishop Hengsbach of Essen, Germany. He pointed out the difference between the present edition and the previous one: a new article on youth has been added, and a clearer concept of the apostolate worked out. For the next few days the Secretary General will be reading the new *schema* in sections, and the council will vote by ballot after each reading as to whether or not to approve. There will be no further debate.

Archbishop Felici warned the fathers that if they expected their votes to be counted, they would have to make heavy enough marks on their ballots for the machine to pick them up. He had previously warned them that they would have to use the magnetic pencils given them for this purpose. "You may have your own splendid new pencils, but they will not make splendid votes." Now he said, "Please make marks vigorous enough to arouse the machine to reaction!"

These days the fathers are often warned that they must be in their seats if they are to vote, but the fathers on their part have long since learned the gentle art of pairing. While one goes to the coffee bar, his neighbor does his voting for him. This of course is not pairing in the ordinary sense, but it is just as effective.

There was no sign of any lessening of discussion when the council turned again to the church in the modern world. Cardinal Shehan made what to me was a most intelligent plea that no attempt be made to separate the natural and the supernatural world too sharply, since the human beings we are talking about live in both, and unify them in one life, not two. It may well be that Cardinal Shehan will be the Elisha to inherit the intellectual mantle of his Elijah, Cardinal Meyer.

Bishop de Castro Mayer of Brazil asked for a better weapon against atheistic Marxism.

Archbishop Morcillo Gonzales, one of the undersecretaries of the council and usually most conservative in his utterances, surprised us by warning that the church should not make the present capitalistic system its fixed economic ideal.

Archbishop Lourdusamy of India warned that a large portion of the world's population has no understanding of urbanization, industrialization, and the other themes which take up the better part of the *schema*. The council cannot afford to minimize the problems of the rural majority of the world's peoples.

One speaker seemed to me to have his feet well planted on the ground of reality—Bishop Mason of the Sudan. Said he, "Let us give the document quick approval. We should not end up with a document so long that no one will want to read it. World conditions are constantly changing: we do not want people thirty years from now to think that we were naïve enough to believe that we could solve the world's problems in perpetuity. The future will have its own problems—and also its own bishops. Let us leave a little to them!"

At about eleven-thirty, which is usually the nadir of the morning session, the moderators asked the council fathers if they did not think it was time to bring the general debate to an end. They did—by a practically unanimous standing vote. Though they followed the custom of balloting on the question of proceeding to the discussion of the individual parts of the *schema*, it was taken for granted that this would also be affirmative, and Bishop McGrath of Panama was asked to make the introduction.

Bishop McGrath, presenting the "introductory exposition" of the *schema*, referred to the decision of the commission to prepare a detailed consideration of actualities today to serve as the starting point for the entire discussion. This was something new for conciliar documents, but since the whole idea of considering the place of the church in the world of today is something new, it was thought not inappropriate. In order not to slant the *schema* too much toward the problems of the Western world, a subcommission had been set up including bishops and other experts from all over the globe, especially from Asia, Africa, and Latin America. Out of their discussions came the introductory exposition.

There was time for only two debaters on the subject thus introduced, one of whom was Cardinal Cardijn, who asked the council to face up to the concrete problems of (a) youth, (b) the workers of the world, and (c) the people of the Third World, that of the underprivileged. He was especially effective in the first category, since he has worked with youth for years. He begged the council to remember that youth make up half the world's population, and the most dynamic half. They differ from the youth of yesterday, for many are cut off from their families and their homelands. They are more united and self-conscious. "They need our help and we should not disappoint them." The old man had to be called to order for overstepping his time, but his is still a voice of power.

➥ *Friday, September 24, 1965*

The talk today is that the long and complicated debate on "The Church in the Modern World," already begun and seeming to proceed with the speed of an inchworm, will actually be brought to a close two weeks from today; that is, October 8. If then another week is left for the *schemata* on "The Missionary Activity of the Church" and "The Ministry and Life of Priests" it will be possible on October 15 to declare a holiday of about three weeks in order to permit the commissions to round out their work. The council would then reassemble for a short month of

voting. The long holiday being so expensive, however, in time
and money, and the business of voting without debates so barren, it is not at all certain that this procedure will be decreed.
We shall simply have to put this down as an eschatological possibility and let patience have her perfect work.

The first action the council took this morning was to send a
telegram to the Pope, through the Secretary General, to felici-
tate him on the occasion of his sixty-eighth birthday this Sunday.

Announced were the results of the vote as to whether to accept the present *schema* on "The Church in the Modern World"
as a fitting basis for further debate or not. The vote had been
taken so late yesterday that the totals were not known when we
broke up. There were 2,111 council fathers who said a resound-
ing YES! against the whispered no of 44 others.

Six were ready to speak on the introduction. Cardinal Frings,
Archbishop of Cologne, made the strong point that the people
of the church should not look with condescension upon the people of the world: the bond of solidarity between the two is the
simple fact that all are men. Others reemphasized the point that
the goodness of man is not enough to save him: "All men have
need of Zeus." (Actually, no one said this, but the line from the
Odyssey came to me as I listened.) Archbishop Elchinger recalled his listeners to the world's demand that the church be
satisfied not with some new declaration on human relations but
that it begin immediately, within its own ranks, to make room
for a maximum of human dignity. This means immediate and
"increasing decentralization in the authority of the church." Just
after this speech, I happened to notice Xavier Rynne and Hans
Küng passing each other in the rotunda—seraphim out of the
pages of Isaiah all ready, as it were, to carry the archbishop's
modernizing words into effect.

The first speaker on Part I of the *schema* was Cardinal
Meouchi, Maronite Patriarch of Antioch. He stressed a point
characteristic of Eastern Orthodox theology, that the resurrec-
tion of Christ is not merely a piece of individual history: it is
rather the starting point of the work of sanctification for the

world, including the whole human race. From that time on the Holy Spirit has been imparting inspiration to such as will receive it. He is, as it were, the soul of the human evolution toward heavenly things. Others emphasized the same general truth and pointed out various particular defects in the text. 1. Men are equal, yes, but we should not forget that individually they differ in intelligence, morality, and physical powers. 2. Let us talk more directly and helpfully to atheists. 3. Cardinal Santos, Archbishop of Manila, in echo of the debate on religious liberty, asked that a too liberal paragraph on the same subject in the current text be deleted, as opening the door to proselytism. 4. Archbishop Ziadé, Maronite of Beirut, in the same spirit as his cardinal colleague, made the interesting remark that the coming of Christ is being more and more realized in the world. This is a conception of the Second Coming that most thoughtful people could accept.

Archbishop Cantero Cuadrado of Saragossa pointed out that in the text on religious liberty the council forbade civil authority to interfere with religion, whereas here it asserts the right of the church to move into the temporal order. He thought that the text could do with a bit more maturity of thought.

This afternoon the English-speaking contingent of the Secretariat and observers met together for an hour. This company is always stimulating, for it takes up subjects in which the members are personally interested and pursues them at a speed impossible in the larger group. Today, for instance, we started on the future of the council and went on to the place of the Pope in the post-conciliar church. The Orthodox men seemed to feel that, since the Pope has not been budged from his primacy, the church is actually structurally unchanged. Others of us felt that with the new possibilities inherent in the synod of bishops, an epochal event comparable to Runnymede had taken place: the king is theoretically as he was, but practically speaking the barons have moved forward. Professor Reid of Aberdeen suggested that this advance in the aristocracy really brought Catholicism no nearer to the democratic Protestant conception (that the Holy

Spirit speaks through the whole people of the church and not through a hierarchy merely) than it was before—but others demurred. Dr. Blakemore cited the new, innumerable, informal contacts between clergy and people which were coming into being everywhere today, calling these as important, from the point of view of the new sciences of administration, as the formal structural relationships of the church.

📖 *Saturday, September 25, 1965*

Today under the generous auspices of the ever-thoughtful Secretariat, we observers visited the Monte Oliveto Maggiore, one of the most interesting abbeys in Italy, not far from Siena, founded in 1313.

On the way home we stopped in the hill town of Pienza, where we were welcomed to the cathedral, museum, and palace by the hospitable bishop of that see.

📖 *Sunday, September 26, 1965*

This morning we went both to the church of Santa Susanna (where many Catholic Americans in Rome go for worship) and St. Andrew's Church (the Church of Scotland here, which many American Protestants attend). This moving from Catholic to Protestant worship in the same morning is always exhilarating and always leaves one with long thoughts. Perhaps it is an exercise to which those who really wish to know the differences and similarities of the two forms should devote themselves more frequently. As has been often said, Catholic cultus is of the eye, largely: Protestant worship largely of the ear. Roman religion, like the halls and walls of Santa Susanna, is populated with saints exhibited in scores of spatial forms. In the Protestant church this morning, on the other hand, there were no candles, no canvases, no statues. Emphasis in the sacramental seems to be facilitated by the visual approach, as the conceptual side of religion seems to go with the aural. The heard word easily takes on the form of Logos and so of logic. At any rate, all the conceptual appeals to the hearing mind were available at St. Andrews: arguments in the Epistles, theologizing in the hymns, and apologetics in the sermon. But all this is slowly changing: Catholicism today is rapidly beginning to appreciate the values of the spoken word of Protestantism, as Protestantism is swiftly beginning to realize the importance of the seen sacrament. Once upon a time all you could be sure of, in going into a Protestant church on a Sunday morning, was that one of your fellow citizens would argue with you at great length, but that day is no more. On the other side, time was in the Roman Catholic Church, when you could be almost certain that you would never encounter anything that would set dialectic thought in motion. But all this is in metamorphosis. This may mean more, in the long run, even than the high pronouncements of the council.

This afternoon, at a point about twenty miles from Rome, the Pope met and conducted worship for a great gathering of gypsies from every part of Europe, the service being followed by gypsy dances. A most imaginative idea.

THE THIRD WEEK

[SEPTEMBER 27 - OCTOBER 1]

✑ *Monday, September 27, 1965*

The council stood this morning to receive the affectionate reply of Pope Paul to the telegram of good birthday wishes sent to him last Friday.

Rumor (a staple product of assemblies such as this) has been to the effect that the schedule of voting would be altered so as to permit a decision on the *schema* treating the relationship of the church to the Jews to come earlier than originally scheduled —but this morning the Secretary General once more read the list of subjects to be discussed and, again, the *schema* in question came last.

Interspersed in the main discussion for the last three days there has been balloting on the *schema* on "The Apostolate of the Laity," paragraph by paragraph. This was completed today, with convincing majorities in favor. Even the votes "yes with reservations" never went above 313—on chapter 3, "Various Fields of the Apostolate."

For the discussion this morning the moderators had apparently picked out speakers whose preliminary résumés had shown that they wished to deliver themselves on the subject of atheism. Some of the contributions to the debate were of the sort with which we in America are fairly familiar in political gatherings where unreasoning orators address followers of like kidney, each being lifted in enthusiasm to the heights of their prejudice by the mere repetition of the word communism. "The voice of the Pope is the voice of only one man: if this whole council will denounce dialectic materialism, the world will listen." "There can be no truce between Catholicism and Marxism."

One Spanish bishop asserted that the protagonists of atheism are the followers of liberal capitalism. If he meant by this that communism is likely to arise in areas where capitalists have used their freedom for their own selfish ends—which was the point made by other speakers—one must agree with him. I gather, however, that he thought the remedy for this kind of situation was fascism, rather than education in social responsibility in a free state. I like to remember that no Calvinistic countries have become totalitarian—probably because they see clearly that though freedom is perfectly to be desired, it cannot be its perfect self unless balanced by social concern.

Against the background of mere denunciation of communism, other speeches, such as that by Cardinal Maximos IV Saigh, Melchite Patriarch of Antioch, stood out in bold relief. Said he, "The approach of the *schema* to atheism is entirely too negative. We cannot hope to save men from atheism simply by condemning Marxism. It should not be forgotten that many who call themselves atheists are not necessarily against the church in its true character; they are simply scandalized by the selfishness of churchmen. We too should be opposed to the exploitation of man by man. To defeat atheism, we had best live out our ideas of Christian brotherhood."

Equally outstanding was Cardinal König, Archbishop of Vienna: "A chief cause of modern atheism is the number of Christians (in name) who do not live up to the principles of Christ. In the face of this the task of the church is simply to show that its members make a more effective contribution to national welfare than does atheism."

For candor that redeems, that releases power, listen to Archbishop D'Souza of Bhopal, India: "The church has not always rightly interpreted the signs of the times. There is Galileo—and also Darwin, Lamennais, Freud, and more recently Teilhard de Chardin. Let us revise our *schema* sweepingly, listening to the voice of God in our time."

All listened attentively to the maiden speech of the new "Black Pope," the recently elected Superior General of the Society of Jesus, the Very Rev. Pietro Arrupe. On the whole, his address seemed to be drawn more from the walled treasuries of conservatism than from the bright vistas of creative thought. He is obviously a man of power. As I listened to him, I thought of the definition of a constitutional statesman—a man of common opinion and uncommon abilities. There was nothing flaccid and weak about his presentation, however: he began with the proposition that the reform of social structures is of the utmost urgency, went on to ask for a concrete and technical investigation of the present status of atheism, and then a militant worldwide campaign against it.

Interestingly enough, the superior general of the Dominican Order, the Very Rev. Aniceto Fernandez, took the rostrum shortly after Fr. Arrupe. Known for his conservatism (and he did say that he liked the scholastic better than the modern approach in meeting the philosophies of the day), he surprised some of us with his ringing denunciation of racial and other discrimination in human society. He pointed out that the remedy for this is the recognition that we were all created by the same God, our Father, and redeemed by the same Christ.

The presiding moderator this morning was Cardinal Döpfner. He kept his eye on the game from start to finish, as usual allowing none of the debaters to overstep either his time or the natural limits of the subject matter.

Now that the first fortnight of the session is over, some of the observers are leaving, many of them to be present at the opening of the universities at which they teach. George Williams was one of those who said good-bye: he is to give the convocation address at the Harvard Divinity School.

Today, and almost every day for the last week, the death of a bishop has been announced, and the council has been led in the "De Profundis" by the senior president. This fact alone should remind the fathers of the changes and uncertainty in the human scene and prevent them, in the *schema* under discussion, from attempting to write down the rules for human society today which will avail, except in general, tomorrow.

There are two schools of thought as to the best way of attacking communism. The hit-it-between-the-eyes company takes for granted that it is thoroughly bad and wants to organize immediately to sweep it off the earth. The other seeks to understand it, and desires rather to attack the evils which give rise to its evil features. One can hardly blame Bishop Rusnack, Auxiliary of the Ukrainian Eparchate of Toronto, for feeling about the matter as strongly as he does, for he has known the grinding ignominy of the concentration camp, being an escapee from a prison whence few came out alive. Nonetheless, the way of patient dialogue would seem to be the better kind.

The company who oppose religious liberty are determined to go down, if they have to, with banners flying. Bishop Llopis Ivorra of Spain said in so many words, "Religious liberty should not be regarded as an absolute good, but only as a good for those areas where Catholic unity does not yet exist." It is not to be thought, however, that all Spanish-speaking bishops belong to yesterday: Bishop Méndez Arceo of Mexico, mentioning hidden sources of atheism, asked the church, in the name of many of his colleagues of Latin America, to make depth psychology a special concern: "The discoveries of Sigmund Freud are equal in importance to those of Copernicus."

I thought Bishop Soares de Resende, of Mozambique, had South Africa in mind when he invited the council, at its close, to make the simple but solemn declaration that all men are brothers.

We were all delighted to see Dr. Cullmann back in his place this morning.

On the whole, it was a dull morning. I thought it the valley of the session so far. Cardinal Döpfner, the moderator, kept all within the ten-minute limit, but by eleven o'clock decibels of private conversation enwrapped the whole assembly. Many were glancing at their watches; and I think that a vote to sink the church and the modern world in the waters of Lethe would have passed by acclamation. The debate this morning was unbroken even by periods for voting. Below us at his desk sat a very bored-looking Secretary General. There was no poetry in the speeches, no longing. I should have been glad to have had a bugler appear in the high gallery every half hour or so to sound a flourish.

The debate on Part I of "The Church in the Modern World" is now ended; and next week should see the end of the debate on the entire *schema*. Everybody, uninhibited by knowledge, seems to be guessing about the further course of the session—and this includes the observers. Last night with Bishop Primeau of New Hampshire as our guest at dinner, we asked about his interesting suggestion that the council, instead of having a long recess of two or three weeks, meet only three days a week, leaving the other four days for the work of the commissions. He pointed out that there is now an added reason for the bishops to have extra time in Rome—for the organization of the various episcopal conferences, which are now to become new and important arms of the church.

At the regular meeting of the observers with the Secretariat this afternoon, Fr. Roberto Tucci, a Jesuit here in Rome who has had an important part in creating the *schema* on "The Church in the Modern World," introduced the second and last part of it by outlining its history: it has gone through many editions.

Edmund Schlink was the first to comment. He pointed out that whereas the Bible speaks of two moments in the life of the Christian, the one in which he is saved out of the world, and the other in which he returns in ministry to the world, the *schema* stresses only the latter. He felt that this would have the effect not only of puzzling non-Christians, who would find no specifically Christian motive in the text, but also of robbing those Christians in concentration camps and elsewhere, where they can do nothing to alter their circumstances of persecution, of a chief source of comfort. Fr. Tucci felt that the text might wisely be corrected along this line.

Dr. Cramer of the Netherlands wished for the *schema* the theological breadth enjoyed by the New Testament, which gives not one view of the world, but a spectrum of views, all the way from judgment to salvation. Fr. Tucci again endorsed a balanced view.

At this point Bishop Willebrands, who was presiding, read a telegram from the papal Secretary of State, sent in behalf of the Pope to thank the observers for their telegram of congratulation on the occasion of his birthday Sunday. This had been dispatched by the executive committee in the name of all of us.

Here Professor Evdokimov of Paris made an intervention of highly nuanced logic which I could follow only afar off—but I heartily approved his conclusion: the married state is not inferior to that of the celibate. Canon Moeller of Louvain, who was also sitting at the head table, indicated that the text at least tries to describe marriage as a Christian vocation.

Professor Caird of Oxford pointed out that in the section under consideration the only words about the size of families were in praise of large ones. He wondered what effect this would have in parts of the world where population is a problem. Fr. Tucci pointed to a paragraph in another section which balanced this to a certain degree, but Bishop Willebrands wondered if both together were sufficient in view of the population explosion.

Metropolitan Emilianos said that in Orthodoxy, marriage is considered an instrument in the mission of the church. Fr. Tucci wished that this might be underlined more in the text. Bishop Willebrands supported the idea with the thought that the new emphasis on marriage as a sacrament, everywhere in evidence in Catholic theology, should find its way into the text.

Pastor Roux of Paris, with the agreement of Fr. Tucci, wished

that the reference to creation in the text might have set it forth
that God created man and woman: the exclusive emphasis on
the idea of man's being created in the image of God is too individualistic.

Dr. van Holk of the Netherlands expressed the feeling that I
have had in reading this and other texts of the council which
have to do with the human situation: he felt that the tragic
choices forced by circumstances upon young people are not sufficiently brought out. They would like to live up to the high
standards of Christian morality, but they cannot. Fr. Tucci was
sympathetic, but thought that the church must stand at all times
for responsible parenthood. (Agreed, but in the meantime, it
should not dream, in its cloistered retreat, that the way to responsible parenthood is an easy one, well marked and without
almost inevitable pitfalls.)

To the question of Dr. Miguez-Bonino of Argentina as to what
response should be given to young people when they ask why
they should be bound by the obligations of chastity, especially
when they love each other, Fr. Tucci gave the answer that there
is no substitute for education in this field. He thought that Dr.
Davidson's question about public housing should be answered
in the section of the text on the economic order.

In introducing that part of the text which deals with war and
peace, Fr. Tucci pointed out that only general principles could
be hoped for, since there was so little consensus on the practical
application of these principles. There is unanimous agreement
that total war is an offense to Christian morals, but beyond that
there seems to be only confusion of voices among the leaders of
the church.

Douglas Steere had prepared a written statement on this part
of the text, copies of which he let some of us have later. If only
all would follow the custom of writing! It saves the time of all:
it delivers the speaker from the temptation to wander, and it
furnishes the Secretariat with a permanent record.

With the two last speeches of the conference—those of Douglas Steere and Professor Skydsgaard—the meeting leaped into

life. One did not need to agree with the speakers wholly to feel the importance of their pronouncements, for they themselves believed passionately in what they were saying. The former praised the council for writing into the *schema* words about conscientious objectors which bring the Roman church into line with contemporary Protestant churches and most modern states. At one point, however, the *schema* seems to add its blessing to national preparations for total nuclear war: its answer to the world's problems seems to be the same as that of the great powers. Fr. Tucci gave no hope that this could be altered, since there is no unanimity among the fathers on the matter. All could wish, he said, that there was a supreme authority in the world which would outlaw war and all the weapons of war—and I myself wonder why this emphasis is not given crowning prominence. If the Christian church could pour life into the slow but continuing human effort to establish government among and above the nations of the world, it would escape being mired in the secondary issue of unilateral disarmament and contribute in a telling way to the solution of mankind's most desperate social problem.

Professor Skydsgaard wished that the text might go back to John XXIII's condemnation of all forms of war. He spoke in English with smothered but contagious emotion. It could hardly have been more impressive in his native Danish. He wished that the last paragraph of the text might be a prayer to God that *if* war comes he may show his mercy in the midst of his wrath and reveal the better way. Fr. Tucci did not think that the fathers were inclined even to concede the possibility of another war: at least they were determined to do and give their utmost to prevent it.

The building up of armaments to prevent war is surely like nothing so much as drinking sea water to quench thirst. Oh for a little daring at this point on the part of the total race! Is there no lesson from the evolution of nature in that those forms of life which have retained their protective armament, like the crustacea, have been far outdistanced by those who have taken the greatest risks?

📖 *Wednesday, September 29, 1965*

The mass this morning was sung—and therefore longer than usual. It was a little before ten when, at the beginning of the business session, Archbishop Felici read a letter from the Holy Father expressing his gratitude for the letter of thanks and good wishes of recent date.

To inaugurate the voting on the *modi* or amendments to the *schema* on "The Bishop's Pastoral Office in the Church," Archbishop Veuillot, Coadjutor of Paris, gave the reasons for the changes proposed. The commission had had it especially in mind to bring the *schema* into conformity to the Constitution on the Church, already promulgated. While protecting the Pope's primacy, they had attempted to make it clear that ordinary power is in the bishops directly, and does not come to them simply as papal aides. The adumbrated reform of the curia includes that of the system of nuncios. To bring the document up to date, a new paragraph was suggested viewing the synod of bishops as already established in principle.

Bishop Hengsbach of Essen now made formal presentation of Part II of the *schema* on "The Church in the Modern World." He outlined its contents in brief—marriage, culture, economic life, the political community, and the problem of peace. On the last subject, as reported yesterday by Fr. Tucci, the commission had been far from unanimous, though on one proposition there was no negative vote: "Any war action which tends indiscriminately to the destruction of entire cities . . . is of itself . . . a crime against God and man." I have no doubt but that this represents the conscience of the world today: I am sorry that the holocausts of Hiroshima and Nagasaki are to be charged inerasably against the United States of America on the books of human history—but the statement in the *schema* refers, of course, only to the future.

Once more the council turned itself into a huge editorial committee, taking up for criticism particular paragraphs in thirty-seven pages of printed text. The moderators had done what they could to bunch the interventions under single themes, with the result that this morning we heard chiefly about matrimony. I had thought that with the Pope's appointment of a commission to study birth control, we should hear little more about that in the council, but no: it is a theme that will not down.

Those who take a conservative point of view on this matter are plainly in a small minority, but no one can call them inarticulate. Cardinal Ruffini, the first speaker, outlined their case well: "Attention could profitably be paid to the traditional distinction between the primary and the secondary ends of marriage, the former being the procreation and education of children, the latter, connubial happiness. The text seems to reverse the order of the two." Cardinal Léger, on the other hand, felt that the text too slavishly accepted the distinction that his colleague had called "traditional," and asked that the end of conjugal love be advanced at least to an equality with the end of procreation. Cardinal Ruffini's formula "can and does express well the end of marriage as far as the human species is concerned. But because marriage joins persons, marriage must have an end for them as individuals."

Cardinal Suenens asked for an amplification and coordination of scientific research in the domain of sex life, in order that the church might have a basis of fact on which to build its moral judgments. He invited cooperation between Catholic and non-Catholic experts.

In the second part of his speech Cardinal Suenens expressed the hope that the council would encourage married couples to renew their vows periodically, perhaps once a year. He thought that more should be said, also, on the value of family prayer.

Bishop Taguchi of Osaka is said to be the only Japanese bishop who takes a conservative point of view on birth control, and this morning, true to his reputation, he voiced objection to the passage in the text which permits married couples to determine the number of their children. He thought it a good thing for children to realize that they had come into being not merely for the satisfaction of their parents but because life had been given to them "out of love and at the cost of sacrifice." Honestly!

Archbishop Zoghby, Melchite Vicar in Egypt, who often says a pertinent word, made a plea for the innocent person abandoned by his (or her) spouse. Must such a person be condemned by the church to live a life of solitude? The Eastern churches have always said no, without prejudice to their doctrine of the indissolubility of marriage. The archbishop pointed out that this way of the East was once followed in the West, and he thought it high time for the West, instead of depending upon the sometimes questionable process of hunting up causes for annulment, to go back to the humane procedure.

Though the debate this morning was somewhat hit-or-miss—including abortion, infanticide, sex education, marriage as contract, the rights of property in marriage, the "pill," and even conscientious objection to war—the discussion was as live as yesterday's had been languid. The dull days are, of course, to be expected and must be taken as they come. Among the fathers, there are men of great, and men of meager, insight: "Few are the mystae, though many the wandbearers." But in any healthy society, even the wandbearers must have their turn: there will be trouble if they cannot say their say.

☞ *Thursday, September 30, 1965*

During the mass this morning one of the bishops, evidently a Filipino, came to the Spanish-speaking secretary, Archbishop Morcillo Gonzales, to show him newspaper pictures of the volcanic disaster near Manila, which has taken the lives of so many

people. They talked with great earnestness and then shook
hands as if the Philippine bishop were just departing for home.
One of our own observers, Dr. Nacpil, whose family is known
to have been in the neighborhood of the volcano, is also returning home, though he has heard that his family is safe. Our prayers go out to them.

The morning was begun by the reading of the introduction to
chapter 2 of the *schema* on "The Bishops' Pastoral Office in the
Church" by Bishop Jubany of Spain. He reported that his commission had made a sincere effort to incorporate into the text
of the document the approximately nine hundred amendments
suggested.

One notices that the paragraphs about the retirement of
bishops still retain their middle-of-the-road character. No age of
retirement is set, but the Holy Father may suggest to any bishop
the desirability of giving up active life. One more headache for
Rome.

The text recommends that bishops get their priests together
for mutual discussions. I have heard it said that the greatest gift
of Protestant Christianity to the Far East is the idea of the
committee; that is, group thinking designed to arrive at a plan
of action: similarly, the greatest single gift of the council to the
church in the field of *aggiornamento* may be the idea of mutual
discussion, crossing all lines of status. Nowhere is the need for
this felt more keenly than among bishops. Up till now the only
lines that have been kept truly open have been those between
each bishop and the Holy See. From now on, however, with the
new authorities being lodged in episcopal conferences, lateral
ramifications will have to be established uniting the bishops in
the several countries through regular meetings and increased
correspondence. I should not be surprised to see the one-day-a-
year gathering of the bishops of the United States increased
three- or fourfold. If a recess takes place in the midst of this
session of the council, it is hoped that the forms of this new
mutuality may be discussed and new programs launched. I judge
from what the bishops tell me that this means more than simply

deciding on the new regime: since the bishops have had almost no experience in the give-and-take of free parliamentary procedure among each other, new attitudes, new amenities, really a new type of government, will have to be developed.

Bishop Jubany referred also to the development of cooperation between bishops and the religious. The text recommends consultation between bishops and religious superiors. This is also a phase of the new mutuality coming into being, which should provide healthier relationships in a field where problems persistently arise.

Going back to Part II of the *schema* on "The Church in the Modern World," the first speaker was Cardinal Journet, who seemed to be answering the suggestion put forward by Archbishop Zoghby yesterday. The cardinal held that the permission granted by the Eastern Church for divorce in certain circumstances was due simply to the influence of the state.

Cardinal Heenan, Archbishop of Westminster, asked that something be put into the text about the praiseworthy practice of adoption and the anything-but-praiseworthy practice of sterilization—but he laid his greatest stress on his main point: since birth control is the really big problem in the sociology of the family, and since the Holy Father has appointed a commission to deal with this adequately, this council is now engaged in a debate on a problem that is beyond its powers to resolve. Would it not be better for the council to give up an attempt foredoomed to failure, omit the whole chapter on family relations, and leave it all to the Pope's commission? As a matter of fact, this is exactly what I expected the council would do. It seems to me that the cardinal has a point: the council can hope to produce nothing more than a haggis of generalities at the secondary level.

The debate went right on, however, the conservatives being conservative and the progressives being progressive.

I marveled at the number of men who, though by their own choice have had no experience of marriage, seemed to come out with a really adequate idea of it. Bishop De Roo of Victoria, Canada, for instance, spoke of Christian marriage as a vocation to seek perfection as a team. "Parents must be the authors of more than physical life: they must be a source of love for the entire family in unfailing and all-embracing generosity." In his mind there seemed to be no nonsense about conjugal love being added as a secondary motive to the idea of begetting children. Begetting children is simply one way of expressing love.

But I marveled that a company of celibates should regard themselves as a court competent to reach profound judgments in this area. As Patriarch Maximos had hinted last year, they really did not know from experience what they were talking about. I was glad that the press was not present to hear and broadcast the remarks of some of the men, who had had only their own imaginings to consult. They not only did not know what they were talking about, but they did not know that they did not know what they were talking about. How do you cure a man of the illusion that he has no illusions? It is partly because of this situation that the Pope's plan for a commission of lay and other experts is much the more desirable one.

Complaints are beginning again that the air in St. Peters is getting stuffy. This seems incredible in such a large hall, but the largeness of the hall is, after all, met by the largeness of the company inside it. I suppose there is a correlation between stuffiness and heat. If, (as Barney Blakemore says) each person gives out 550 BTU's per hour, and in moments of high emotion 650 BTU's, it was fair this morning to use the latter figure to compute the animal heat being imparted to the basilica. That figure times 3,000—the number of the people here—gives a fairly torrid total, with a corresponding figure for air vitiation.

We celebrated a new first today. Fr. Daniel O'Hanlon and Fr. Frank Norris, our two American translators, had an arrangement installed whereby they can talk over wires to their hearers in the observers' tribune. When, at the next Vatican Council one hundred years hence, an instantaneous translation system is installed for all, the bishops can thank for it the pioneers, Frs. O'H. and N. of the Secretariat for Christian Unity, way back in 1965.

Mass this morning was said in the Syro-Antiochian form. The melody of the chants and responses was pleasing to the ear, and every now and then, even exciting—but there was no harmony. Nor is there any harmony in the Roman rites that we have been using at this session. This gives to them a flavor of antiquity, to be sure, but it is hard for me to understand why, in this day and generation, worshiping congregations should confine themselves to the gaunt Gregorian mode (perfect as it is in its own moment) and deprive themselves of the riches of polyphony. I remember an old Jewish legend which says that when Satan was asked what he missed most after he had been cast out of 'heaven, he replied that it was the blowing of the trumpets in the morning. At this session, I miss most the full-voiced hymn *Christus vincit* of the earlier sessions.

I find that I have not been converted to long and intricate rituals. It is so much easier to add a form than to dispense with one, once it is established, that the old churches now show the overweighting effect of a kind of ecclesiastical Parkinson's law. I believe that even God likes men who have something to say, say it well, and then do not go on decorating it.

The council was silent this morning, at the beginning of the session, to hear the Secretary General announce the October calendar. It could not be absolutely definite, he said, in view of the fact that the fathers have such freedom of speech, but it was probable that there would be a short recess for the week of October 17—"a recess from morning sessions," he said, "and not a recess from work, for the commissions will be busy, and so will the episcopal conferences." This latter is especially signifi-cant: the Pope will give them their agenda, but the whole process of organizing to handle the agenda will be new to many of them—a new first in *aggiornamento*.

On Monday next, when the Pope will be leaving for the

United Nations, the mass will be offered for the success of his journey, and on the following day, at the end of the morning congregation, the fathers will await the Pope's return and receive him in St. Peters, probably about noon.

At the end of the morning the Secretary General read to the council a résumé of the speech that the Holy Father is to make to the United Nations. He intends specifically to include the council fathers in his greeting to the UN, and he will praise the UN for its unremitting attempt to establish peace on the basis of human dignity. Of course his presence will mean even more than his words: it will tell the members of the UN that the Roman Catholic Church is solidly behind them.

Cardinal Spellman was not in his seat this morning: he has apparently left for New York to serve as John the Baptist to the Pope.

After four more speeches on The Family this morning, the debate was closed. Little has been said on the subject this year which had not been said last year. Cardinal Gracias, Archbishop of Bombay, just this week returned to the council, summed up for me the position of common sense when he asked that the final text be left to laymen.

Cardinal Slipyi followed. In a wandering disquisition he spoke of many things, seeming to be chiefly critical of communistic governments, at whose hands the old man has suffered so long and so grievously.

Bishop Ddungu of Uganda, speaking for Africa, asked for a far stronger text against racial discrimination. Bishop Hacault, Auxiliary of St. Boniface, Canada, made an interesting comment on polygamy, pointing out that though it is far from the union of love among equals, which is Christian marriage, it does yet lend stability to certain societies and should rather be called imperfect than condemned outright.

The discussion now moved on to the subject of the church in its relation to culture, approaching it at a fine high level in the persons of such men as Bishop Schmitt of Metz, Bishop Elchinger of Strasbourg, Bishop Lebrun of Autun, Archbishop-Elect Pellegrino of Turin, and Bishop Blanchette, director of the Catholic Institute of Paris. These men said that the church should realize that God is speaking to it through the modern world, and should acknowledge in the text that it owes not a little to that world (Schmitt). The church should treat the world as a companion, realizing that men outside the church have built up their own secular theology, as it were, even including messianism. It must not ally itself so closely to older cultures as to be unable to understand the modern ones. Too often it labors to give answers to questions that are no longer being asked. In every nation of the world there should be a top-level institute at which the church and the best surrounding culture could meet for creative dialogue. (This from Elchinger, always on the front line.)

The importance of sports was underlined. Attracting an ever-increasing number of spectators, they constitute a part of our modern mentality. They have an aspect of beauty; they bring out courage, team spirit, and other virtues; and not least, they give people of different social levels the opportunity of meeting together and uniting their interests (Lebrun).

Applause greeted Pellegrino, for this was his maiden speech since his appointment as archbishop. He wanted the text (a) to make a high place for the science of history, quoting Professor Skydsgaard on the need for a common study of the history of salvation, and (b) to come out strongly for freedom in scientific investigation. I thought it a good day for Italy when he received his appointment. Bishop Blanchette supported him in his plea for a stronger word about the study of history. He observed that this would deliver the *schema* from its naïve optimism—which seemed to suggest that everything would be put right in the world with a bit of mutual goodwill.

For the last two or three days, votes on "The Bishop's Pastoral Office in the Church" have been interspersed in the debates, all of them highly favorable. Next Monday will see a vote on the total *schema,* and one more piece of legislation will be ready for promulgation.

THE FOURTH WEEK
[OCTOBER 4-10]

ᐍ *Monday, October 4, 1965*

The Pope had left early this morning to meet with the United Nations in New York—an event of which the council was fully conscious. A beautiful prayer for his safe return, for the United Nations, and for the peace of mankind was circulated in print before the mass and used in the course of the service. The service itself was a special one, including an anthem by the choir— in harmony. In the midst of all the chanting we have been having lately, all in simple melody, the blending of the voices of basses and tenors came as a welcome and most refreshing relief.

There were only five presidents present this morning (Cardinals Liénart, Frings, Ruffini, Siri, and Alfrink), the others having gone, I take it, with the Holy Father. Cardinals Agagianian and Lercaro were absent from the moderators' dais, and from the secretaries' table we missed Archbishop Felici himself and Bishop Kempf.

Cardinal Liénart took the place of Cardinal Tisserant; and Archbishop Krol of Philadelphia, the place of the Secretary General.

There were six more speakers this morning to hold forth on the subject of the relation of the church to the modern world. Archbishop Morcillo Gonzales thought that the second chapter should be turned over to a post-conciliar commission to give it better structure, bringing human culture into harmony with Christian culture through the formula that though culture is the work of man, it is God who endowed man with the intelligence by which he develops his culture. Bishop Frotz, Auxiliary of Cologne, wanted a great deal more said about the place of woman, emphasizing the complementary relationship of the sexes, not only in marriage but in social life as well, including the religious orders. Others spoke of the danger of making natural science a norm for theology: from it, it is impossible either to prove or disprove the existence of God. The church's great debt to science was stressed, but so also was the crucial decision now being forced upon science as to the right use of its tremendous power.

For the first time in the history of the council we had this morning a touch of the give-and-take with which we are familiar in ordinary gatherings in the West. Before now we have heard one council father commenting upon the address of another, but this morning we had a comment on a comment, for Archbishop Zoghby, smarting a bit under Cardinal Journet's animadversion that his (Archbishop Z's) previous plea for the innocent person in a broken marriage suggested the capitulation of the Eastern Church to the state, now expressed his sorrow that the Eastern fathers should be accused of accommodating their teachings to political interests. He pointed out that he had not asked for divorce but had only put in a humanitarian plea for some special dispensation for the innocent and unfortunate victim of a marriage wrecked by a consort.

The morning was about a third past when discussion was opened on chapter 3 of the second part of "The Church in the Modern World"—economic and social life. The fathers did not seem to like it very much. Cardinal Siri cautioned the council not to go beyond its competence. He was strongly supported by Bishop Hengsbach, who spoke out of his experience of the great industries at Essen, and by Bishop Hoeffner of Münster, who spoke in the name of eighty German-speaking bishops. They pointed out the naïveté of the *schema's* pontifications on agriculture, monetary policy, the right to strike, and other matters about which experts disagreed.

At least three speakers called for the formation of a council for social action at Rome, which would assist similar councils throughout the nations of the world. This reminded me of the fiery days of the 1930's when in the Congregational Christian Churches of the U.S.A. we went through a similar debate which finally resulted in the formation of the first such church council. Perhaps I should add that if the Catholic bishops as a whole knew about our subsequent history of controversy over our own council for social action, there would not be quite so many votes favoring it. But only the brave deserve the fair: I would hope that enough of them would discern the immense preponderance of tangible benefits (in the education of the people to social needs) over possible dislocations and disasters within the framework of the church to approve the proposal with gusto.

A Spaniard and two or three others thought that liberal capitalism—by which I take it they mean capitalism without any state control whatever—is rapidly becoming obsolete. Archbishop Fernandes of Delhi, speaking for more than a hundred bishops of India and elsewhere, begged the council to remember that the problem of the underprivileged is the—simply *the*—problem of humanity today. He damaged his argument in my mind a little by observing that many people seem to be putting too much stress on the limitation of populations. Others thought that the text should treat more fully of the role of the state in social planning, social security, and the proper balance between work and leisure. One other thought that the *schema* stressed too much the rights of workers, and too little those of owners. How familiar! Clearly the Roman Catholic Church needs no council for social action to develop controversy on such matters.

One of the men suggested that the whole chapter be turned over to the new synod of bishops. If indeed the bishops in synod assembled might from the outset cultivate the habit of keeping their windows open upon human society, the Roman Catholic

Church would not sit in the world as the aged grandparent of modern civilization, but as its partner, its blood brother.

📖 *Tuesday, October 5, 1965*

All the arrangements this morning were directed to the return of the Pope and the council fathers who had accompanied him. We observers sat not in our accustomed place, which was relinquished to the diplomatic corps, but in a corresponding tribune on the southeast side of the rotunda. Again Cardinal Liénart acted as senior president, and Archbishop Krol as secretary. Since Cardinals Tappouni, Wyszynski, and Lercaro were here at the beginning of the session, and Bishop Kempf did not enter at the end of the morning with the papal entourage, it was evident that none of them had gone to New York.

There remain for debate the last three chapters of "The Church in the Modern World." This morning there were still ten to speak on the third chapter, on the church and economic-social life. I culled the following bits from their presentations.

Capitalism and communism have the same source: individualism—and both are wrong because they are not based on the primacy of the human person.

The value of production is to be measured by the good it brings to man: the goal of unlimited production is too materialistic.

Emigrants should not be forced to give up their own culture in order to accept the culture of their new land.

People in such countries as the United States and Australia, where workers have made great advances, should remember that most of the workers of the world still live amid horrible injustices.

Man's work is participation in the work of God, but the greater his power over nature grows, the more he must learn to control himself.

Progress is not only a fact: it is a right.

The social conscience is everywhere beginning to come to birth, unfortunately not always because of the teaching of the church but often because of the teaching of Marxism.

The farmers of the world are in desperate need; the revenues from agriculture are too small; young people are moving to the cities everywhere. The whole world should be concerned for the farmer not out of charity or pity, but out of sheer justice, since the world lives on the product of the farm.

Once more three of the fathers, perhaps in a concerted effort, called for the establishment of an international secretariat to educate the church on the world's social needs and to give the church's witness to the world in the field of social justice—an "international council for social action." For years, of course, the National Catholic Welfare Conference in the United States has issued most enlightened statements on critical social problems, and I dare say that this organization has had its counterpart in other nations as well, but the proposal now is to establish a coordinating group in Rome which, being international, would stand at a higher echelon of influence than any merely national committee. We learned this afternoon at the meeting with the Secretariat that this proposal had been made through the commission framing this chapter, that it had been decided not to incorporate the idea in the text, but that with the developing interest the commission might now make the proposal its own. I pray a little private prayer that if the new secretariat is actually set up here, it will not be so reactionary as to dim the vision or blunt the edge of daring of such forward-looking organizations as the National Catholic Welfare Conference.

Chapter 4 of the second part of "The Church in the Modern World"—on political life—called only four fathers to their feet to speak.

One of them, the Spanish bishop Beitia, still reverted to the religious-liberty theme. There is an ailment in this city called

"Roman throat" which makes swallowing difficult: there is obviously in this council a vigorous minority that has Roman throat
when it comes to swallowing the idea that vis-à-vis the state,
other religious communities must have the same rights as the
Roman church, even in a "Catholic country." Bishop Beitia asked
if this chapter might not be a good place to assert the right of
the state to make a public confession of faith—which (if I understood him correctly) would give the church that made the same
confession a standing not enjoyed by the others. Perhaps it was
only a plea for a state church, but it seemed to have further overtones.

Bishop del Campo of the same country asked for just tax laws,
and underscored the moral obligation of citizens to obey such
laws and not try to cheat their own government.

Archbishop Baraniak of Poland thought that the council ought
to help the faithful living under anti-Christian governments by
setting the boundaries beyond which they ought not to go in
cooperating with such governments.

Archbishop Hurley of South Africa, speaking in the name of
seventy bishops, nobly said: "Let us speak less of the rights of
the church and more of the rights of man."

Two speakers inaugurated the discussion on chapter 5—war
and peace. Cardinal Alfrink of Utrecht made a specially strong
presentation: "The very possession of arms is a danger. When
many nations are heavily armed, it is inevitable that a 'balance
of terror' should arise. Wars are not inevitable: the church should
support studies of their causes which can lead to their final elimination from the face of the earth."

At about 11:30 the first contingents of the diplomatic corps
began entering the building to take the seats we had left them,
but the debate went on. Indeed, at noon, when it had been
hoped that the Pope and his companions would be entering the
basilica, it was announced that his plane had just touched down
at the airport. He did not finally arrive till about 12:45 when,
led by the choir, we sang a psalm of praise as he walked the
length of the nave to take his place at the center of the presi-

dents' dais. A brief greeting was read to him by the acting president, Cardinal Liénart, and he responded in kind. It was a historic occasion. This was the first time a reigning Pope had ever set foot on American soil. As the Pope himself had said, on arrival there, he now renewed the gesture of the discoverer Christopher Columbus, when he planted the cross of Christ on that side of the Atlantic. He had left here yesterday morning, made eighteen speeches in the course of his visit, and was now back at midday of the second day. As he left the hall, we all sang *Christus vincit*, the great hymn that has become almost the hallmark of the council owing to its frequent use at other sessions but which has not been heard at this session till now. The bishops made up for their long omission of it by giving it all their voices in a concentrated sacrament of volume and meaning.

At our meeting with the Secretariat this afternoon, Fr. François Houtart of Louvain introduced chapter 3 of Part II of "The Church in the Modern World"—on economic-social life—and answered questions about it. He thought it not as dynamic as it might have been, but hoped that it might be improved.

The discussion was sprightly, due largely to the fact that so many participated, speaking briefly and to the point.

Emilianos: The text would be stronger if it began at the beginning to stress Christian stewardship. Houtart: This has actually been mentioned in the first part. Willebrands: The real difficulty is that, even with the presupposition of Christian stewardship, it is not easy to know how this should be expressed in modern times.

James Norris: Note that the text does indeed condemn the wrong use of wealth, without condemning wealth itself.

Findlow: Social advances in England in the last century were due largely to the "Christian Socialists." Today a good deal of the progress asked for in the *schema* has already been achieved in advanced countries, but on a secular basis, wealth still being the main objective. What is needed is the spirit of the Christian Socialists, who put God and man before wealth.

Staack: Is it true, as the *schema* says, that those who are in dire need may legitimately take from the rich? Houtart: Yes, according to the old idea of the church—but perhaps the statement in the *schema* is not sufficiently guarded. It is designed not as a norm for individuals so much as a philosophy for social revolution—which, of course, is better if it is not violent. There is no hope for many nations in South America, for instance, if a better distribution of wealth is not arrived at—and this the church should sanction.

Lawrence: Would it not be better to write into the *schema* the "Lund principle" that the various churches should not do separately what they can do together? Houtart: Yes. The *schema* now suggests this course for exceptional cases, but it might well be strengthened.

Davidson: Should not the *schema* suggest how better to use leisure time? Houtart: There is a short allusion to this in another spot, but even there no practical suggestion.

Pawley: In South America the church is regarded as necessarily reactionary: would it not be well for this chapter to have a penitential introduction? Houtart: Agreed. There is something along this line elsewhere in the *schema,* but it might well be placed here also. Willebrands: But we must not be too ready to take a holier-than-thou attitude to our forefathers.

Cramer: God has often been seen as the guarantor of the social status quo, and this connects us with the past. He should also be seen, however, as the creator of things new: this can connect us with the future. And again, work has been the chief function of man, but now the demand for it is decreasing and man will have to find a new function. Houtart: An excellent idea for post-conciliar thinking on this subject.

Caird: Nature is not for the use of man without limitation. He must use his stewardship to protect nature. Chemicals that kill wildlife, for instance, should in many cases be forbidden.

Reid: It is apparently the Roman Catholic teaching that an individual may refuse to participate in some particular war, though not in others, but today conscientious objection is against all war. Should not this difference be brought out in the *schema?*

Willebrands: I question whether the Roman Catholic attitude toward conscientious objection is as you have described it. Certainly conscientious objection to all types of warfare has been accepted by the church.

Now the company turned to the *schema* on the missionary task of the church, which was introduced by Fr. Congar. Outlining the different theories of missions held in various quarters of the church, he noted that the majority of the commission had come round to the idea that the entire church is missionary, with its missionary task differing in various situations. He coveted for the *schema* the same spirit of missions as is evident in some of the documents of the World Council of Churches.

Turning away from the old motive of "snatching brands from the burning," the church now finds its missionary impulse in two sources: (a) sheer service and (b) the desire to realize God's plan of bringing people into self-conscious unity in a visible church. He thought that the role of non-Christian religions in God's plan had been unwisely avoided in the *schema*.

Cullmann: In these days, between the first and second appearances of Christ, the church is in a missionary period: the preaching of the gospel prepares for the last days.

Vischer: The current edition of the *schema* is an immense improvement over its predecessor but (a) the Holy Spirit should not be identified as the "soul" of the church as an institution (but Houtart later commented that he thought that the church in the passage referred to was actually the whole people of God); (b) "Go ye into all the world" was said to the entire church and not to the bishops alone (but Congar thought that this referred both to the apostles, or bishops, and to the whole church); and (c) though promising words are being said about cooperation on the mission field, the text might well make practical suggestions for achieving cooperation (and though Congar agreed, he thought that a preliminary period of experimentation would be called for).

Petros Selassie: Has only the Roman Catholic Church the right to preach the gospel in public? Congar: Though I believe that all churches should preach to the non-Christian world, such men

as Cardinal de Arriba y Castro say that the apostolic church is
the only one with full right to preach the gospel. This is a question not yet resolved by the *magisterium* or teaching authority
of the church.

Lawrence: Being a lawyer I realize that the word cooperation
may be used either in a strong or a weak sense: how is it used
in the *schema?* Those presiding thought that it was meant to be
understood in full strength.

Vajta: The division of the church produces anguish in truly
sensitive Christian souls: should not this come out in the *schema?*
Congar: Actually, ecumenism in the Roman church takes its rise
from the mission field, where this anguish is most acutely felt.

📖 *Wednesday, October 6, 1965*

This morning we were back to normal.

A first vote was on the *schema* on the pastoral duties of bishops, which has now gone through the entire conciliar mill and
is today, thanks to a vote of 2,167 to 14, ready for transmission
to the Holy Father. At the next public session of the council,
with or without slight touchings up by the advisers to the Pope,
it will be ready for solemn approval and promulgation.

Now the council was to have laid before it for voting the
amendments to "The Accommodated Renewal of the Religious
Life." These words need translation out of the dialect of ecclesiastical Rome. "Accommodated" really means brought up to
date, and the "religious life" means the life of those in orders.
The amendments were introduced by Bishop Compagnone of
Anagni, which is not far from Rome. No less than 14,000 of them
had been submitted, but these fortunately, because of duplica-
tions, were reducible to about 500. The text is now edited with
a view to conciseness. The religious are encouraged in every

way to get back to the spirit of Christ and the founders of their orders while at the same time they make themselves familiar with the needs of the modern world and ask themselves how Christ and those founders would themselves have attempted to meet those needs. It is suggested that instead of multiplying new laws, they strive through prayer and activity, in cooperation with the church at large, to cultivate a new and dynamic spirit. The bishop interpolated into the printed *relatio,* which was in the hands of us all, a paragraph on institutes, which are a relatively new kind of organization whose members dedicate themselves to the works of the church but do not withdraw from the ordinary life of the secular community. In general, the whole work of adaptation to today is the responsibility of competent superiors.

This morning began a spiritual war against the lukewarmness of the chapter on war in the *schema* on "The Church in the Modern World." In general the speakers wanted to see it lifted out of its milk-toast state and given such toughening as would make it a useful instrument in the real world.

Cardinal Liénart began it by begging that the text should not make too much of the difference between a just and an unjust war, since the means now used for any kind of war on a large scale are inhuman.

This was followed up by Cardinal Léger, who, with the streamlined modernity of the very instruments of destruction he condemned, made four points: 1. The *schema* should be a solemn condemnation of war. The classic rules for limiting warfare no longer hold. 2. International authority needs to be developed into dominant strength: the *schema* would do well to give its main support to this. 3. The passages on conscientious objectors should be changed, so that they would not appear to have a soft and timid character. 4. The Roman Catholic Church should cooperate with all who seek peace, especially with non-Christian religions such as Buddhism.

Cardinal Duval, Archbishop of Algiers, called nationalism an outmoded antiquity.

Archbishop Garrone of Toulouse drove the point home that peace is not simply absence of war, and true love of peace not simply a cloak for fear of war. Peace should be waged by doing away with the conditions that lead to war.

So it went—and it was noticeable that this morning there were a larger number of interventions by English-speaking fathers than usual—Abbot Butler, Bishop Wheeler, Auxiliary of Middlesborough; Bishop Marling of Jefferson City, Missouri; and Bishop Grant, Auxiliary of Northampton, England. They felt that it was immoral for a nation to mass together great quantities of arms with the intention of wiping out whole cities with them. They did not like the text reference to "the legal presumption" that for a soldier, the order of a superior officer is always right. They were clear upon it that the nations of great wealth must help the undeveloped nations to come to maturity economically, intellectually, and spiritually. And they all agreed with Cardinal Léger that it is silly to think of all conscientious objectors as morally second-class.

Bishop Simons of Indore, India, supported by Bishop Marling, made a surprise move (and a singularly telling one, in this context) in favor of birth control. Pointing out that the growth in populations is a fruitful cause of war, he asked that some means be discovered for checking growth in population. "The conclusions of many theologians need to be rethought. The traditional arguments against birth control based on the frustration of nature are not at all convincing. The sense and binding force of the law prohibiting all artificial means of birth control are open to doubt and, according to our basic juridical principles, a law on whose meaning grave doubt exists is not binding."

Four men called again for a strong central church organ for the protection and promotion of peace.

Only one man—from Spain—seemed to want to move a little slower than the others; and the debate this morning ended with Bishop Brezanoczy of Hungary asking for a "solemn, clear, grave, and absolute condemnation of nuclear warfare."

On the way home I stopped off at the Vatican Radio building

for a radio interview with Fr. Kieser, who is in charge of national broadcasting in the United States for the Paulist order.

▬ *Thursday, October 7, 1965*

This morning mass was led by an Argentinian bishop—and I say "led" advisedly, for he easily led the field, coming in at least half a sentence ahead of the rest of us in every prayer.

The theme of the debate being still War and Peace, the morning had an auspicious start with the speech of Cardinal Martin, Archbishop of Rouen. He made seven brief points. 1. Though this *schema* discusses a matter of life and death for men, and even for mankind, the style is completely lacking in spirit. 2. In practice there is no difference between an offensive and a defensive war: preparation for either involves the piling up of arms and creates the volcano on which we are all living. 3. There may have been a difference between just and unjust wars in the days of the past, but now that total war is with us, it is a distinction between what is inhuman and what is more inhuman. 4. The very notion of war as a means to solve international difficulties should be banished from the human mind. 5. Christians should take the lead in a universal movement for peace. 6. Machinery for arbitration should be set up. 7. The way is long, but we must set out upon it immediately.

What a contrast this is to the Roman Catholic philosophy I knew fifty years ago, when the priests in my neighborhood all took the attitude that war is inevitable, do what one might!

The great speech of the morning, if not of the session, was made by Cardinal Ottaviani. Though he had a manuscript in front of him, he did not look at it (for, alas, he is almost blind); and his Latin came out with the strength of a river in flood. The gentle quaver which his old age lent to his Ciceronian style made

it most moving to all his hearers—and a fitting vehicle for the heroic substance of his utterance. He asked for a total ban on war,
and a great deal more attention to the means of forestalling war—
education at every level, international brotherhood without distinction of race, color, levels of culture, or anything else, a fair
distribution of the world's goods, and (we could hardly believe
our ears) a continued battle against totalitarian governments.
Sanctions must be organized to punish disobedience to the developing international government of the world. We should not
be deceived into thinking that guerilla warfare disguised as "national liberation" is anything but warfare. "Just as we hear of
plans for a united Europe, and as we have the United States of
America and the United States of Brazil, why cannot man reach
the point where there will be only one united world republic,
one common fatherhood for all men?"

The happy combination of youth and maturity in one mind
was not lost on the audience, and Cardinal Ottaviani received
the first applause which has been given to any intervention this
session.

Others spoke well, too, calling for a stop to colonialism, pointing out that there is no such thing as a "minor war," asking for
a merging of our fractional national interests into an international whole, and demanding far better guidance from the
schema as to what public authority may do or not do under
pain of losing its right to obedience.

Birth control came up again, under the heading of the population explosion leading to war. This time it was Bishop Gaviola,
of the Philippines, who took a negative and reactionary view.
One of his arguments was to the effect that the theory that the
world might become overpopulated might lead the faithful to
doubt the wisdom of God in his creation. (I thought of the Scot
in my first parish who would never allow his wife to have a
simple operation which would have permitted her to bear children on the ground that if God had wanted her to have children
he would not have created the need for the operation.) He
thought it better for governments to give subsidies to families

rather than to attempt to limit them. Cardinal Caggiano seemed to be nodding in approval.

Bishop Carli devoted his whole intervention to conscientious objectors, to whom he has not a little conscientious objection. His basic argument was that, given a just war, public authority must have the means of acting in self-defense.

When now Cardinal Suenens asked the council if it did not consider that the subject had had sufficient discussion, I was surprised at the unanimity of the vote for cloture. So the famous *schema* 13 on "The Church in the Modern World" goes back to the commission laden with a backbreaking number of amendments in the hope that it can be reported out in from three to six weeks in acceptable shape. One has the impression that the fathers in their eagerness to bring the council to an end are now ready to cut the debates short and vote approval of anything that is not absolutely intolerable. A no-fooling mood has settled over the assembly. Lighthearted jokes seem to be fewer—and I have not heard a single limerick about any man or event in this session.

Cardinal Agagianian now introduced the Very Rev. John Schütte, Superior General of the Society of the Divine Word, who gave the *relatio* of the new text on the missionary activity of the church. He recalled (and who could forget) that at the previous session the fathers had demanded, instead of the few jejune paragraphs that had been presented to them, a full-size treatment of missionary activity in the church—and as a result he now submitted what they were about to discuss. The new and enlarged text speaks of the end or purpose of missions, of today's opportunity, nay, necessity, for them, of the direction and coordination of missionary activity, and of the missionary duty of every one of the people of God. The *relator* spoke in full, even copious, praise of the Congregation for the Propagation of the Faith—and waited for applause, which came. It took no depth psychologist to tell the hearers why this laudatory excursion had been made, for immediately afterward came a description of how it was proposed to reorganize the curial control of missions by setting up at Rome a special body that should provide dynamic leadership and not merely administrative acumen for the missionary enterprise—and made up of people personally familiar with the mission fields themselves. The speaker asked for a system in which the dioceses should give without being begged to give for missions. He felt that the present *schema* might become a Magna Charta for the enterprise. Applause followed his presentation.

The four speeches that ended the morning all approved the proposed *schema* in general, but each one had in it a strong *tamen*—BUT. They thought that more should be said about saving faith; about proselytizing activities, especially in South America, where the Pentecostals are active; about the work of the Holy Spirit, who is at the very source and heart of all missionary activity; about the judgment of God upon all who hear the gospel; and about the need for cooperation among all Christian groups.

Cardinal Santos spoke his great gratitude in the name of the Philippine hierarchy to all who had expressed sympathy for their people on the occasion of the recent volcanic eruption in the Islands. The Australian episcopal conference, and the bishop and diocese of Guadalajara, Mexico, had sent generous gifts of money as well.

ꙮ Friday, October 8, 1965

This morning we had a Coptic mass. It is not for me. Incense was freely used most of the time, and I felt that a good deal of the smoke got into the minds of the worshipers. At least there was little in the rite of sufficiently bright color or conception to appeal to the intellect in its higher reaches. The non-Western scale of the music was interesting—for a while—but the motifs were repeated so everlastingly that I thought it comparable, in the realm of liturgics, to doggerel in that of literature. The sanctus came out strong and genuine: let us at least say that kind word. I thought that in general the rite cried out for *aggiornamento*.

A new list of votes to be taken on the *schema* on priestly training was passed out this morning. There is apparently a good deal of criticism of this one, which the new plan for voting will help to pinpoint.

Another *schema* that makes the liberals throw up their hands is the one on Christian education. We heard one bishop say the other night, "It would be all right if they would change the title to 'Principles for Catechizing Infants.'" There is a movement afoot to vote this down, even at this eleventh hour, on the ground that it is better to say nothing at all about the matter than to say something so trite as to attach it to 1865 rather than 1965. From our part of the stands we shall be watching to see whether this cry of *"Pereat!"* is responded to. In the present let's-get-home-soon mood of the council it may not be, and if it is not, the decree will simply share the fate of that other harmless but useless declaration on the Media for Social Communication and slip sweetly into oblivion.

"Please stop sending around circulars!" asked the Secretary General once more. This practice is not only against the laws of the house but now seems to be interfering with the distribution and collection of votes.

For the last three days the debate has been laminated with votes on the *schema* on "The Accommodated Renewal of the Religious Life." These have been almost unanimously favorable to the amendments suggested: the largest number of negative votes any one of them could muster was 57—which gave permission, under certain circumstances, to ordain lay brothers to the priesthood. On Monday there will be a vote on the whole *schema*, duly amended.

The debate on War and Peace was continued by those who had won the privilege by securing seventy others to second them. This was still at a high and clear-seeing altitude. Monaco stressed the human right to emigrate. Tivoli in Italy wanted to set up the banner of brotherly love over the whole text. Down-and-Connor in Ireland added in the same vein that the greatest gift which the council could make to mankind was precisely the message of brotherly love in the gospel. But I thought the honors of the occasion went to France. This part of the debate was begun by Bishop Ancel, Auxiliary of Lyons. He gave a ringing call for an unqualified ban on war. "Even psychological war is unchristian." Like the Pope in New York early in the week, he called the nations to accept a genuine international authority, adding the note that this would not be opposed to authentic patriotism, though it would be the genuine enemy of exaggerated nationalism.

And the discussion was closed with the memorable words of Bishop Boillon of Verdun. "Three times in the course of one century France has been the scene of destructive warfare. Our text is so laced with distinctions as to make it almost ineffective. It speaks of conventional arms as though they were not really destructive: in the diocese of Verdun 1,300,000 people lost their lives in conventional warfare. The distinction between belligerents and non-belligerents means nothing today when the implacable law of modern warfare calls for maximum destruction with a minimum of delay. The distinction between minor and major wars is likewise valueless. Let the nations heed the Christian call to international humility, which will accept limitation of sovereignty; and to international poverty, with richer nations helping the more needy ones; and to international meekness of heart, which will enable all men to battle against injustice." In concluding he referred to the twenty women of various nations and faiths who, in a religious house near here, are living without food and in a discipline of prayer that the council fathers may have light as they deliberate on this most awful of human social problems today.

The bishop spoke to the hearts of his hearers because he spoke from his own heart, and while he was speaking I saw again the scene of Verdun, which I had visited just after World War I.

The trees were all shot away: on the ground one could turn up used shells, old machine-gun belts, and sometimes the bones of men; it was on that spot that a brilliant high school pal of mine had lost his life. We tend to forget scenes like this, which scream with the madness of war—or we get used to them. I remember a missionary woman saying, amidst the horrid degradation of certain Alaskan Indians, "I can't keep my horror keen enough!" So it is with us all: we dismiss from our memory the sight of writhing pain, the sound of gargled blood. I owe a debt to the Bishop of Verdun for recalling to me the terrible memory of his tortured hillsides.

Now Archbishop Garrone summed up the discussion on *schema* 13. He pointed out that the document constituted a first attempt at working out a new language of dialogue between the church and the modern world. He assured the fathers that the Latin would be improved and the whole thing shortened. He noted the several criticisms, now that it was too philosophical, now too oblivious of supernatural law, now too optimistic, now too static; and on behalf of his commission he promised a studied attempt to bring it up to higher standards.

With this, the *schema* on "The Missionary Activity of the Church" was again picked up, and seven bishops had their say about it. They thought that its main subject should be the missionary activity of the entire people of God; that though the love of God lay in the heart even of non-Christians, it was there only in a beginning and imperfect form and that the text should declare it; that the document should give a much higher rating to the life of the religious on the mission field; that some mention should be made of the persecution of missionaries; that the Blessed Virgin Mary as the Queen of the Apostles should be acknowledged the special mother of missionaries; that the sacrament of confirmation should be defined as the moment when a baptized layman becomes an apostle; that the presence of evil in the world should be stressed; and that an invitation should go out to all missionaries, Roman and non-Roman, to collaborate with one another to the limit permitted by their churches.

All of these comments were constructive and tended to support, rather than discredit, the substance of the document.

This afternoon we held a meeting of our English-speaking contingent. As our Catholic members were not present at the beginning, we were slow in getting at the nubs of controversy, but ideas finally fed upon ideas and it was not easy to break up at 5:30. We talked of virtually everything except ships and sails and sealing wax—including the status of mixed marriages (on which Rome has not as yet given any definitive lead), cooperation on mission fields, and proselytism (with plenty of illustrations supplied by Dr. Holt of South Africa and Dr. Miguez-Bonino of South America), and the *schema* on revelation (which is so replete with questions that we are going to take it up again at our next meeting).

Saturday, October 9, 1965

At the end of this afternoon most of the English-speaking observers went to the library of the Church of Santa Susanna, the American Catholic Church in Rome, to enjoy the tea that was served and to provide an occasion for a bit of publicity for the small library which does a quiet but efficient piece of work.

Sunday, October 10, 1965

This morning we worshiped at the Methodist Church and late this afternoon went to the radio center of RAI (Italian Radio and Television), where we participated with Richard Senier on two of his panels, Mildred on one discussing women in the church, and I on another having to do with the observers at the council.

THE FIFTH WEEK
[OCTOBER 11-16]

✍ *Monday, October 11, 1965*

At the end of a sung mass this morning, we enjoyed another motet by the choir. We are doing better on the congregational responses, now that we are getting used to them, and I rather think that the Lord of heaven has learned to endure them; but I can picture him opening the windows of heaven to hear better when the choir sings its motets.

This morning we were reminded of the past, for this was the third anniversary of the opening of the council by Pope John XXIII—but even he, with all his clairvoyance, could not have imagined how strongly and unexpectedly the church would have forged ahead in her thinking in the course of these three short years. The council fathers voted this morning on the whole of the amended *schema* dealing with the renewal of the religious life 2,126 to 13—and one more document was ready to be presented to His Holiness for final touches before the final vote, and final promulgation. She moves.

Most of us were thinking, however, of the immediate future, for this is the first day of the last week of scheduled debate. Five more days—seventy-five more speeches—and this phase of the council will be history. I tighten my belt and determine not to languish on the last lap.

Voting on the *schema* on priestly training was introduced by Bishop Carraro of Verona. He indicated that since the previous draft had been approved by a good two-thirds majority of the council, the commission had paid no attention to any amendments that were in conflict with the original text. The commission had, however, tried to adapt it to the spirit of the Constitution on the Church. It had described education for celibacy in a positive and constructive way. And it had tried to leave room for different types of training according to the varying needs of different parts of the world.

The council now reverted to the theme of missions. Let me make a compote of six of the first seven speeches of the morning.

More emphasis needs to be placed in the *schema* on the need of fervent prayer to God through Mary, Queen of Missions. (You have guessed right: this was from Cardinal Ruffini.) In the *schema* certain roles seem to be conferred on all the members of the church which really belong only to the hierarchy (again the Sicilian archbishop). Certain non-Christian religions contain elements admirable in themselves, but which can find genuine completion only in Christianity. We and our missionaries should always be ready for dialogue (Cardinal König). We must get it out of our heads that Christ came for a small chosen company of people: he came to the world. Now that the episcopal college is formally established, all bishops must regard all missions as their responsibility. It may be well for missionaries to have standing not only in the dioceses from which they go but also, at least temporarily, in those to which they come (Fr. Quéguiner, Superior General of the Foreign Missionary Society of Paris). One third of the human race, because of the wall of persecution, is prevented from hearing the preaching of the gospel, and the young generation is growing up in atheism. Arrangements should be made to broadcast catechism courses and liturgical services. And incidentally, the Congregation for the Propagation of the Faith should not invade the area of the Eastern Churches, but leave that to the Congregation for the Eastern Churches (Bishop Sapelak, Apostolic Visitor for Ukrainians in Argentina).

Bishop Gonçalvez da Costa, of Mozambique, thought Christian schools a good, if not the best, instrument for missions; and Bishop McGrath, of Panama, called on the one hand for emphasis on the missionary responsibility of the entire people of God and, on the other hand, for pointing up the specific responsibility of bishops in this regard. He thought that all those in charge of mission areas should be consecrated bishops.

Archbishop Cordeiro, of Pakistan, the seventh speaker, in the name of more than fifty bishops of various nations gave what I thought to be an especially attractive, and true, presentation of the raison d'être of missions. In a sense, the missionary motive is centered in the good of man, but more accurately speaking, its primary center is the glory of God. Just as the sun's rays go out through all the solar system, so the glory of God's love must be carried to all mankind. This is what lends the Christian mission its happy urgency: a Christian animated by God's love finds nothing so delightful, nothing so positively exhilarating, as carrying that love into the world.

Now the tenor of the morning's procedure was interrupted by the reading, by Archbishop Felici, of a letter from the Pope to Cardinal Tisserant, the senior president of the council. It had come to the attention of the Holy Father that certain of the council fathers wished to bring up on the floor of the council the question of the celibacy of the clergy in the Latin church. It seemed right therefore, that His Holiness should make his own views known without prejudice to the freedom of others to share their views with the rest. He thought it was *not* expedient to have a public discussion of a topic of such delicacy and of such far-reaching importance to the church. Here applause interrupted the reading. The Secretary General went on: "If any of the council fathers would like to make observations on the subject themselves, it is suggested that they do so in writing. Such communications, addressed to the council presidency, will be examined with great care by His Holiness. At the conclusion of the reading of the letter, there was extended applause, but its meaning was ambiguous. Was it because the Pope had negated the idea

of public discussion of celibacy in the priesthood or because he
had invited observations about it? Posterity will never know.

I have the same special qualifications to discuss celibacy as any
celibate has to make a judgment about birth control, that is,
just about none at all; but the untold enrichment of my life and
ministry through intimate companionship with womanhood at its
noblest leads me to think that there is far too much celibacy in
the Roman church. Some day the question will indeed be discussed in high quarters here and some form of pluralism established.

The discussion was closed by four more speakers, of whom I
shall quote only Archbishop Attipetty of Verapoly, India, because he spoke so nostalgically the language of yesterday. Said
he, among other things, "The council gives the impression of using its collegiality to excess as though it were trying to impose
on the Pope its own method of reorganizing what is really a
part of his own personal secretariat. And surely it would be
well to include in the text reference to St. Thomas Aquinas, the
prince of the philosophers of the church, in order to show the
direction which missionary teaching should take." By this I was
reminded of a parody one sometimes hears at the English College, which begins, "Should auld Aquinas be forgot, and never
brought to mind?"

📖 *Tuesday, October 12, 1965*

It was a dull day overhead today, and the same kind inside St.
Peters.

A letter was read from Cardinal Tisserant to the Holy Father
informing him that his wishes concerning the celibacy of the
priesthood would be carried out. Applause at the end indicated
the agreement of the council fathers.

Announcement was made that the next public session would be held October 28, the anniversary of the election of Pope John XXIII to the Papacy. Mass that day will be concelebrated, with prayers that the results of the Pope's peace mission to the United Nations will be fruitful. The Secretary General announced that many of the council fathers (many? the total count of them without exception) were interested in learning what the calendar of the council for the next few weeks would be—to which he could only reply, "Patience, brethren, patience!" The best dopesters say that it will close on a day somehow sacred to the Blessed Virgin. This might mean November 21 or December 8. I have been hoping for the former, but Cardinal Heenan, next to whom I sat at lunch today in the English College, tells me that it is almost certain to be the latter, since the report from at least one of the commissions has not been asked for till December 1.

The debate today was somewhat leaden, partly because it dealt in the technicalities of the organization of missions and partly because there was not a little repetition.

There were, however, some new thoughts offered. Missionaries must learn the art of being missionaries—of discovering lay apostles, animating existing apostolic organizations, inspiring zeal in others, and the like. Although native leadership is rightly taking over on mission fields, the necessity for supplying missionary assistance has not waned in the least. The *schema* should not remain silent about those missionaries who are not called to spend their entire lives in missionary activity, some of whom are diocesan priests sent for a time to relieve a missionary diocese badly in need of clergy. In fact, it would be profitable for dioceses with an excess of clergy and funds to accept mission territory for their own development. Priests and the religious on the mission field should never be found doing what laymen can do equally well. The term propaganda has come to have such a disagreeable connotation that it might be well to rechristen the congregation *propaganda fide* as "The Secretariat for Evangelism."

Let me pick out three speeches for special mention. Arch-

bishop D'Souza of Bhopal, India, said that he would forgo reading his speech and simply present it to the council Secretariat.
If applause could have crowned him, he would have sat down
with a diadem. Father Arrupe, Superior General of the Jesuit
order, whom we are to entertain at the "Observatory" (the place
where most observers live) tomorrow night, gave a bristling hand-
ful of reasons why missionary activity is often ineffective: the
story of missions is frequently designed for children, is too sen-
timental, breathes the spirit of Western superiority, is myopic and
superficial; missionaries have been selected for good health and
mediocre talents; and too much of the time of our best men has
been taken up with money raising. Bishop Lamont of Southern
Rhodesia spoke last. He is the one who last year described the
original missionary *schema* as so many dry bones and, more than
any other single speaker, compelled its re-editing and amplification. Once more this morning he used language imaginative and
telling. "The *schema* is not a document intended to console missionaries but to bring the church up to missionary passion. No
land is so primitive as to be unfit for the gospel nor any so civilized as not to need it. As Peter the Hermit organized the Cru-
sades, bishops must today organize the missions of the church."
Applause.

This afternoon at our weekly meeting with the Secretariat, a
number of speeches were made by a number of men in a constructive attempt, like that of the council fathers, to impart to the
schema the life and zest which should belong to a commanding
missionary document. Participated: Staack, Miguez-Bonino, Mar
Athanasius, Lawrence, Abba Petros Selassie, Solomon, Schlink,
Eapen, Maan, Stransky, Girgis, Blakemore, El Pharaoni, and
Vajta. Bishop Willebrands led the discussion and Père Congar
supplied the running commentary.

Many felt that the missionary *schema* stands too stark and independent, and that it would be given power by being more
closely connected with the greater declarations of the council,
such as those on the church and on ecumenism, even quoting
from them where necessary. Many felt a special weakness in

the ecumenical dimension, a lack of a good basis on which appeal might be made for cooperation with and from non-Roman Christians. Some echoed thoughts that had been voiced at St. Peters, asking for a description of the distinctiveness of the gospel as compared to the values in other religions. Others pointed to instances of cooperation already established, and to areas ready for it. One speaker mentioned the denigration of other Christian churches in some of the books and teachings of the Roman church in certain countries, and hoped for improvement.

And in this last realm the Paulist Fathers in the United States certainly deserve the palm, for they are putting out a series of books on non-Catholic groups to be used by students in Catholic high schools—and written by representatives of the groups themselves! This, I believe, is something new under the sun, a by-product of the council itself, having been engineered here last year by Fr. Bader.

I thought the speech of the afternoon was made by Fr. Stransky who, though a Catholic, compared the document before the council with corresponding documents issued by the World Council of Churches and various other confessional families. He found in it no idea of building up the *human family* through the church. "We do not seek the amelioration of mankind in order to promote the gospel: the improvement of the lot of man is itself an expression of the gospel." Again, he thought it entirely too restricting to confine missions to work in foreign countries, seeing in the Protestant erasure of the line between home and foreign missions a more realistic approach than that envisaged in the *schema*.

📖 *Wednesday, October 13, 1965*

The council did a distinguished piece of juggling this morning, keeping four balls in the air.

First, there was the *schema* on priestly training. Being put to a vote, it was accepted by 2,196 fathers, only 15 voting no. So another piece of legislation goes to the Pope to be readied for final promulgation.

At the very close of the congregation, the juggler threw a second ball into the air: Archbishop Marty of Reims introduced the *schema* on "The Ministry and Life of Priests." Debate upon this, the last of all the *schemata* to be discussed at this council, will be begun tomorrow. One might judge from this that the council was about ready to draw down the shutters and go home—but no: the Secretary General, having read only a fraction of the list of those who want to participate in the debate, made the unwelcome announcement that at least one more day for discussion would have to be added to the schedule. The council will therefore surely meet on this Saturday, and possibly even on next Monday, which was to have been the first day of recess.

Add to this the unexpected emergence of ten men who had secured seventy backers for speeches in the already closed discussion on missions (the third ball to be tossed up) and it will be understood why so many of us put up a prayer that the Holy Spirit would swiftly descend upon the assembly and persuade the fathers to deny themselves the luxury of last words. But this is a prayer no one expects to be answered: just as all the substitutes on a college football team want to be called into play during the last moments of the last game of the season, if they have not played before, so, many fathers who have not previously spoken want to be counted as vocal participators in this historic event.

The speakers this morning made the point that like Paul, who did not want to preach where Christ was already known, lest he build on another's foundation, missionaries should not enter territory already occupied by other Christian bodies; that the *schema* has so much to say about the missionaries that it tends to neglect the local clergy and the local people, who are the missionaries' chief support; that the missionary institutes (which we Protestants are likely to call mission boards and their constituents) must simply work out better relations with the churches at home and the churches abroad (and where have I heard that before?); and that though the apostle Paul might refer to money as "filthy lucre," no missionary can get along without it. With governments everywhere now withdrawing salaries formerly paid to sisters from the sending countries in order to make room for the employment of native teachers and nurses, it was especially necessary to provide a steady source of income for the missions. This might be provided by annual contributions from all dioceses according to their means, with some more prosperous dioceses even adopting missionary dioceses in toto.

Notable was Fr. Degrijse, Superior General of the Congregation of the Immaculate Heart of Mary, popularly known as the Scheut Fathers. In calm and clear Latin he called for grass-roots ecumenicity on the mission field, that the great hopes fostered in the ecumenical movement would not be dashed. In words which almost echoed what had been said by the observers at their meeting yesterday, he noted four stages of cooperation: (1) friendly understanding and association, (2) the common use of radio facilities, hospitals, schools, and the like, (3) cooperation in the fight against such public evils as racism, public immorality, and (4) cooperation in the actual work of evangelization, provided there be no danger of confusing Catholic and non-Catholic norms.

As I reflected on this speech, the clearer became my conviction of the enormous influence which the Secretariat for Christian Unity and the other progressives have had upon this council. The *schemata* on which they have concentrated their attention have come out as worthy utterances of a great church. Those which have neglected their point of view will, I believe, be bypassed by posterity. The commission on missions could have had an open door to their influence, but in the printed *schema* there had been little evidence of its infiltration. In the speech of Fr. Degrijse, however, seconded a little later by Bishop van Cauwelaert of the Congo (who gave us the memorable sentence: "Too much prudence in ecumenical cooperation may prove the greatest imprudence"), one could feel the spirit of the new day entering into the missionary area. Bishop Gay, of Guadeloupe, also gave the idea his support.

One man, Bishop Velasco, of China, just to keep the matter in balance, called for the old-time religion with its emphasis on individual salvation. He did not like to hear too much talk of an ecumenism that is essentially false. (Fundamentalists, wherever they are heard, have a charm of their own.)

For factual information I found the intervention of Bishop Han Kong-ryel, of Korea, especially illuminating. He spoke of the four possibilities open to an individual who wishes to follow a missionary career: (1) he can go out as an individual under the sole authority of the bishop on the field; (2) he can go out under a missionary society (where conflict with the bishop's jurisdiction may arise); (3) he can be assigned by his own diocese on a temporary basis to a missionary diocese; or (4) he can join a society (or properly "institute") to which a mission territory has been turned over by the Holy See—so that there is no question of dividing authority with a local bishop. The speaker pointed out the difficulties attending each one of these possibilities and asked that the *schema* set forth the principles that would serve to meet them.

Fatigued from the long debate, we were shocked into delighted attention by the appearance in the ambo (or pulpit) of Eusèbe Adjakpley from Togo, a lay auditor. He was as black as espresso, and clad in a kind of toga with shouting orange and black stripes, he was an impressive figure. His speech was pure fresh air, in French. Africa's very presence in the council, he said, is an indication of what missionary endeavor has done. He spoke of the regions in the world where the church is scarcely present, and those which are becoming radically de-Christianized: "In the world of today mission is everywhere needed." He spoke of the eagerness of the laity in their own vocations, and of youth, especially in the vocation of building up a civil society, to throw their strength on the side of Christ and the church—if and when they are touched by the proper influences. He minced no words about the need for ecumenicity: "All believers are called to work together." Would that we had more of Mr. Adjakpley everywhere!

The debate was summed up by Fr. Schütte, Superior General of the Society of the Divine Word, who thanked all for their proposed amendments to the text, including those in the auditors' and observers' tribunes who had been good enough to make suggestions in writing. This is the first time that the contributions of the observers in this area have been mentioned.

The *schema* on "Christian Education" introduced by Bishop Daem of Antwerp, was the juggler's fourth ball. There has been an undertone of criticism of this *schema*, as I have hinted, on the ground that it is entirely too naïve. I doubt, however, whether this will assume the shape of formidable protest. So far as it goes, the *schema* is not bad in itself—and the fathers are not seeking further controversy. The bishop indicated that the comments of the fathers, so far as possible, had been incorporated in the text. Some appeared still to believe that the commission had been "soft" (as they said) in its treatment of the relation between church and state; but after long discussion of the subject, it had been concluded that the *schema* would be strongest, and truest to the mind of the council as a whole, if it came out simply but firmly against the idea of monopoly of education by the state. Some had asked for a privileged position for Thomas Aquinas in education—and he had now been accorded fuller mention.

Perhaps, given the modern temper, this is all that can be done for Thomas today. We do not need to copy him slavishly; but if genius is brought to expression by taking fire from genius, then the human race will always be blessed by keeping contact with his incomparable mind. I suppose that Aristotle was the greatest thinker of the ancient world, and in St. Thomas he rose from his tomb with the New Testament in his hand.

📖 *Thursday, October 14, 1965*

Though the question of the celibacy of priests is not to be discussed at the council, it seems to be capturing the headlines elsewhere. The International Episcopal Conference of the bishops of Latin America, for instance, has announced that it has sent a telegram to the Pope declaring its solidarity with him. At the American press conference held here in Rome every afternoon, celibacy has been a subject for discussion three days running. In the French newspaper *Le Monde* appears a letter from a Brazilian bishop to the Pope asking for some relaxation of the regulations in view of the shortage of priests in his country.

A final vote on "Christian Education" was taken this morning though, as I have said, there was considerable opposition to it —on the ground not that it was evil, but simply weak—and as prognosticated, the negative forces assembled relatively few votes —183 out of 2,096.

The discussion of "The Ministry and Life of Priests" this morning took the shape, for the most part, of a number of little packages of good advice to priests. The Spanish cardinal, de Arriba y Castro sounded a note which is seldom heard in Protestant Christianity: "Priests should live a holier life than laity." With Protestants, it is a different life, but not a holier. The virtues of the priest are those of the good shepherd—zeal, pastoral concern, magnanimity, love for all, especially the poor and sinners, perfect patience, constant availability and perseverance, and all based on a fervent interior life, built about union with Christ. Manual labor is not prohibited to priests, provided it can be made a witness to Christ. I liked one bishop's beautifully scholastic way of putting it: "A true priest enjoys an ontological configuration with Christ the priest."

Cardinal Meouchi, Maronite Patriarch of Antioch, gave the *schema* a quick but searching review from the angle of Orthodoxy. It is too Western, hardly recognizing that the priest in the East lives quite a different life from his brother in the West (being married, for instance). It is too juridical, lacking spiritual thrust. It is based on a certain rigidity of principle, which makes it useless for changing times. The relation of the faith of the priest to the efficacy of the sacraments is not made clear, nor is the fact of the power felt by the priest as a member of the total priesthood. And not enough attention is paid to the necessity of study for an understanding of the mentality of today. On the whole, this was the most searching of the commentaries made.

(I discover that I am building up a simple theory why the Uniate churches in the eastern Mediterranean seem to be making such inroads on Orthodoxy and why Orthodoxy smarts under the rivalry. Rosenstock-Huessy once remarked, "The Western Church was able to outgrow the ancient world: the Eastern Church never did, but got moored permanently at the exit of antiquity." The Uniate craft among the latter, captained by Meouchis and Maximoses, seem ready to weigh anchor and so find it easier to attract crews.)

Cardinal Ruffini made several interesting observations. "The text appears to say that the apostles set up bishops in the early church but no priests. This is contrary to the explicit testimony of the book of the Acts." This might have been regarded as a weakening of his strong call for episcopal authority, had he not gone on to say that the priests about a bishop should never overstep the consultative function, lest this lead to a collegial government within the diocese—a horrendous idea. He felt that each priest should make frequent confession, utilizing the aid of a spiritual director, and that groups of priests living together should organize themselves in some sort of discipline, putting one of their number in charge. Echoes of the celibacy question had evidently reached him, for he praised the *schema* for its strong insistence on an unmarried priesthood.

After the third of the twelve speeches this morning, the debate was interrupted to make room for Cardinal Bea's introduction of the last *schema* to be voted on this week—that on "The Relationship of the Church to Non-Christian Religions," including Judaism. He pointed out that the text stresses the matters which unite Christians to men of other religions and so build mutual fellowship. The Roman Catholic Church now for the first time proposes fraternal dialogue with leaders of the great non-Christian faiths.

As for the section on the Jews, which has of course caught the attention of the world more than any other, he repeated the point which he had made many times before, that there is nothing in it which should be construed as having a political character. (Though everyone knows that as soon as it reaches the state of Israel and the environing nations, it will become a political instrument.)

1. The text now has it that the church *deplores* hatred, persecution, displays of anti-Semitism, directed against Jews at any time and by anybody, and to some this seems weaker than the statement in the previous edition, which declared that the church *condemns* such practices. The cardinal said that the former word was used, since the word condemn is restricted in ecclesiastical documents of this sort to heresies. The council mutters in its beard about this one, as does the world outside.

2. The Secretariat on Christian Unity (which is the commission that composed this *schema*) proposes that the expression "guilty of deicide" be eliminated from the text, though the substance of the idea be retained in the sentence: "Although the Jewish authorities and those who followed their lead pressed for the death of Christ, nevertheless what happened in his passion cannot be attributed to all Jews, without distinction, then alive, nor to the Jews of today." The cardinal gave as the reason for this the fact that the word *deicide* is misunderstood in many regions—and it does, to be sure, drip with various emotional connotations.

The truth is that this part of the *schema* has already had woven into it so many threads of controversy that it is impossible now to expect clean-cut approbation. Members of the commission have made innumerable trips to the Middle East to secure the judgment of the wisest leaders, and as a result the present text is the best that can be hoped for. It will probably attract more noes than any part of any recent *schema,* but my guess is that it will pass, partly because the council is tired of a controversy that seems to be out of control and fruitless.

📖 *Friday, October 15, 1965*

In contrast to the early days of the council, these last days see so many women in the auditors' tribune and in the transepts of the basilica during the debate that they are taken for granted. It is hardly possible to believe that their appearance at a council of this sort is absolutely new. At the next council, more will be seen of them—though not without the opposition of those whose philosophy reads, "Fundamentally standeth everything still." Recently the National Council of Catholic Women in the United States held a series of meetings in which, though an ordained priest conducted the mass, women did such other things as it was thought appropriate for women to do, such as reading the Bible, receiving the offering, and the like. Promptly the curia, on hearing of it, laid a ban on all such female sharing in the mass. This was part of the background of the intervention prepared by Archbishop Hallinan of Atlanta, which he was not able to give on the floor of St. Peters, time for discussion having run out, but which he has now given to the public press. It advocates the participation of women in all church services for any office not reserved for the hierarchy. It is reasonable and comforting to reflect that, thanks to the mills of God, the way of Atlanta will one day be commonplace.

The mass this morning was that of the Antiochian Maronites.

Though there was no harmony in the music whatever, the melodies were strangely alive, in contrast to the other Near Eastern rite of last week. Except for some brief but apparently very old phrases, only the Western scale was used. It was used, however, with such exciting intervals and such unexpected changes in time, to express joy or solemnity, that, though I could not understand a word of the Syriac or Arabic, I found it a renewing experience.

When the Secretary General began to announce the calendar for the next few weeks, all held their breath but, alas, he was able to give us no details beyond November 18. Congregations will be completely recessed next week, and the first week of November, and there will be public sessions on October 28 and probably on November 18—but for the rest, including the naming of that portentous day of closing, silence.

The discussion of the morning was very like that of yesterday, replete with good advice for priests, especially that they should cultivate holiness. Cardinal Döpfner thought the text of the *schema* read too much like a book designed for pious reading. He thought that priests today would not be particularly happy to read that they are "a precious spiritual crown for the bishop," in view of the fact that priests have come a long way since the time of Ignatius, the original author of the saying. Others also emphasized the fact that the priest today lives in a new world. Cardinal Alfrink thought that the *schema* virtually locks the priest up in the church and sacristy, when it should be opening many doors for him into the world—doors to hospital visitation, to dialogue with all sorts and conditions of men, to studies whereby he might explain to his people the problems of modernity and how to meet them. Others, like Cardinal Landázuri Ricketts of Lima and Bishop Tomé of Mercedes, Argentina, urged caution at this point. The fear was that a priest's activities outside the church would rob his people of his more important services at altar and confessional. "The obsession for so-called 'incarnation' in the present-day world has tendencies to get out of bounds."

Several practical suggestions were made. Cardinal Herrera y Oria, Bishop of Malaga, asked for houses in which priests and deacons could have at least a year's study of preaching, simple preaching—and he also wanted a trained sociologist available for every seminary.

Archbishop Miranda y Gómez of Mexico City was true to his North American ideals. He believes in planning one's work, and then working one's plan. He would like to see a good pastoral program set up for every diocese, if not every parish, involving not only the bishop and his priests but also the religious and the laity, who would approach their problems as a team. He cited instances of such well-organized spiritual campaigns in Mexico which had resulted in a revitalizing (and restructuring) of the dioceses. Archbishop Nabaa of Beirut, one of the secretaries of the council, made a strong, down-to-earth plea for paying priests decent salaries. Though they are ready to serve the church in a spirit of poverty, it is not good either for them or the church that their minds should be filled with a nagging concern for the means of keeping alive and well.

An ecumenical thread bound many of the speeches together. "Our separated brethren should not be treated as unbelievers." "Orthodox priests and Protestant ministers have given eloquent witness through martyrdom." I thought of a word of Coleridge: "Rivals [rivales] are only those who inhabit the opposite banks of the same stream."

The vote on the amended schema on "The Relationship of the Church to Non-Christian Religions," including Judaism, was taken this morning, and at the end of the session, the result announced. There were 250 noes, a large number for any of the more recent schemata, but far below the one third of those voting and present necessary to defeat passage. So the checkered history of this schema in the council draws to an end. On the whole I believe that church historians will regard it as an enlightened piece of legislation.

One pleasant, family feature of the council will never get into the church histories. There is a man, a retired canon of St. Peters,

well on his way into a gentle senility, who wanders about the
hall every day, talking to anyone who will listen, always followed by the eyes of many. He is assigned a special seat but
obviously does not like sitting. Today the Secretary General had
a long talk with him, as he has had before. It is, in fact, the
way he is treated by the secretary, moderators, presidents, and
others, that gives one an affectionate feeling toward the council.
Instead of being annoyed at him, as they well might, they listen
to him as patiently as possible, steer him to safety when he is in
the way, and in general handle him as they would their grand-
father. One virtue of this council lies in its humanity.

📖 *Saturday, October 16, 1965*

Yesterday evening my wife and I had the pleasure of being
received by Cardinal Heenan at a tea given by him at the English
College for the observers and their friends; and this morning
in St. Peters I enjoyed his address on the life and ministry of the
clergy. He took as a kind of text a quotation from Gregory the
Great, "The care of souls is the art of arts." He spoke of the
Legion of Mary as an impressively effective society wisely ad-
ministered by laymen advised by a sympathetic and prudent
priest. Frank Duff, the founder of the society, is here as an auditor and was greeted with applause when the cardinal mentioned his name. With good English balance, the cardinal asked
for priests who, without giving up their own inner life, saw
something of their fellow priests ("It is no waste of time for
priests to play a round of golf together") and their fellowmen in
general ("It is better to preach the gospel to people of God than
to stay at home to write books and articles about them"). Applause at the end, ordinarily forbidden, showed that the council
agreed with him.

I was happy to be able to recognize the Very Rev. Fr. Arrupe, Superior General of the Society of Jesus, as the celebrant of the mass this morning.

Actually the session this morning was an extra one, added to permit further discussion on the life and ministry of priests; and it was evident from the content of what was said that this is a subject of genuine concern to the bishops. And cardinals!—no less than eight of whom participated.

Today, like yesterday, it was impossible not to detect an undertone of reference to a certain malaise among the priests in some, if not many, parts of the world. There are priests who seem to be unhappy with the kind of obedience that is expected from them by their superiors. These would have been happy to hear a repeated insistence this morning that bishops must divest themselves, in mind and deed, of every shred of what Cardinal Shehan called "episcopalism," the virus that turns bishops into dominating lords instead of collaborators. Some priests, lapsed from their high motivation, need to be brought back by the tenderness and sympathy of fellow priests. The trouble with many is simple loneliness.

I do not remember that the matter of celibacy was brought up in connection with this loneliness, though it might well have been. References to celibacy did, however, creep in at many points, so that one might almost say that there was a refracted discussion of it, in spite of the Pope's letter.

Cardinal Bea looked at the subject squarely. He noted that though the text admits in one place that celibacy is not required by the very nature of the priesthood, it seems to deny this in another passage. He asked that no unique claims be made for celibacy, else what of the married priests in the Eastern churches? Are they not priests in the fullest sense? He received a bit of applause at the end, and needed no more, for the council had given him its highest tribute—silence while he was speaking. It is indeed remarkable that the council has learned to listen so intently to some of its more prophetic members that when they rise to their feet to speak, the light hum of submerged conver-

sation, which is a veritable part of the architecture of St. Peters
during ordinary debate, ceases and all hearts throw out a car-
pet of quiet in expectation of receiving a word of insight.

One speech that the council will remember was given by the
ever-delightful Bishop Leven of San Antonio. I wish that I could
reproduce it verbatim. "A voice must be raised in behalf of 'the
forgotten man' of Vatican II; namely, the assistant pastor. It is
laughingly said that he does have one right—that of good Christian burial, but this is no laughing matter for the assistant pastor himself. Though these men have reached adult age, they are
often regarded as adolescents still in the seminary. We do not
exploit their talents. Modern industry would never spend large
sums of money to train men and then ignore them afterward.
Assistant pastors should by right be the first consultants of the
pastors, and not be regarded as guests in the rectory." The clapping of hands registered the approval of many fathers.

Not read by Bishop Leven, but part of the typewritten speech
that he let some of his friends see in advance, was a plea for
the use of good office machines in the larger parishes. He de-
cried the absorbing of the time of an educated person by cleri-
cal duties that modern automation makes simply unnecessary.
This was surely in the best American, not to say Texan, tradition.

The Roman Catholic Church feels a certain sanctity about the
priesthood which is seldom encountered in the contemporary
Protestant church. For one thing, the priest keeps himself "sanctified" by constant celebration of the Eucharist. The Protestant
minister of the right sort also tries to keep himself a pure chan-
nel for the flow of God's grace into human life, but he has no
single, palpable, universally recognized vehicle to this end, such
as the mass. The priest's danger lies in confusing the essential
grace with the vehicle which carries it, whereas the minister's
lies in losing the grace in the absence of the tangible vehicle. It
seems obvious that we need each other at this point, for neither
flexibility nor solid structure can be dispensed with.

Twelve of the morning's sixteen listed speakers having spoken, the moderators asked the members of the council if they thought the time for closing the debate had come, and called for a standing vote. All such votes for cloture have been almost unanimous, and this was no exception. Ballots were immediately distributed to determine whether the council accepted the text as a basis for further elaboration, and before adjournment the calculating machines had given the answer—1,507 ayes, 12 noes. (It will be seen that at this extra session over a quarter of the council fathers had absented themselves.)

And in our observers' tribune this morning there was only a Gideon's band—Fairweather, Grotoff, Roux, Schmidt, Petros Selassie, Mosconas, Thurian, Vajta, and I, along with five men of the Secretariat, Frs. Davis, Corr, Long, McConnon, and O'Hanlon. All the rest had gone off on an excursion to Rieti, a region sanctified by memories of Francis of Assisi—but the temptation of being present for what may be the last day of debate of this history-making assembly was too great to be resisted by some of us.

And we heard noteworthy declarations. "Today's priests must be the soul of a new world that is now rising" (Cardinal Rugambwa of Tanzania). "The parish can no longer be regarded as a tiny walled city, like a medieval monastery. Today's parishes must follow their people wherever they go" (The Primate of Quebec). "There must be one poor man in every parish—the priest" (Cardinal Florit, giving expression to a sentiment widely held, especially in France and Spain). "Sacred eloquence needs to be restored to its pristine splendor" (Bishop Bank, of Hungary). And one can only hope that the last words spoken in the debate (by Bishop Ndongmo, of the Cameroons) will long linger in the episcopal mind: "We bishops must remember that the Holy Spirit often speaks through those who are beneath us in authority. Priests are not to be treated as minors: the quality of the laity of the church depends chiefly upon the quality of our priests."

So one phase of the great council comes to an end—the debating phase. Or at least it probably comes to an end, for speak-

ers who succeed in finding seventy seconders will be allowed to
say their say a week from Monday, after the seven days of recess. It has been made as hard as possible, however, for them
thus to spin out the discussion, for they must turn in their completed speeches, no résumés being allowed, by Monday next.

I cannot say that I am sorry to see an end to the debates, but
as I think over the total experience, I find myself full of admir-
ing appreciation of the health-giving effect of such talk. Sheer
talk among the council fathers—not only the public talk in St.
Peters but the private talk at meals, in the lounges, on the way
to and from the Vatican, everywhere—this has had its salutary
effect. By airing their thoughts, especially their grievances, the
fathers have felt a wholesome freedom (and I remember the
good philosophy of the applejack makers of old New England:
it is better to sizzle at the bung than burst a hoop), and by ex-
changing their insights they have come to new depths of dis-
cernment about themselves and the church. The talk has been
positively nourishing—and the consequences will be bracing in
every diocese.

For the week of recess, Mildred and I fly to Athens, exchang-
ing the grandeur that is Rome for the glory that is Greece.

THE SIXTH WEEK

[OCTOBER 25-29]

📖 *Monday, October 25, 1965*

After a busy but delightful week in Athens, Mildred and I came back to Rome yesterday to discover that during the recess at least two events worth recording had taken place.

On October 18 the Vatican had announced that "The Relationship of the Church to Non-Christian Religions," which denies that the Jews were ever collectively guilty of the crucifixion of Christ, will be finally voted on and officially promulgated by the Pope, along with the other *schemata* now ready, three days hence.

The revised text on religious liberty had been given out in the course of the week, and this morning it was introduced, for voting tomorrow, by Bishop de Smedt of Bruges.

I think now, as I thought when first I heard him, that Bishop de Smedt is not surpassed in presenting a case clearly and convincingly. This was the sixth time he had appeared before the fathers to speak on religious liberty for the Secretariat for Christian Unity, to which had been assigned the duty of preparing the text of the declaration. He made the special point that religious liberty does not free either an individual or society from responsibility for recognizing and practicing true religion. Religious liberty is a legal guarantee protecting men from being

115

prevented from seeking religious truth. In an illuminating simile, typically Smedtian, he compared religious liberty with a citizen's liberty to have a car: his driver's rights are protected by traffic regulations, but these do not exempt him from driving prudently as he makes his way through the city streets.

The foundation of the right to religious liberty, said the bishop, is the dignity of the human person, the fact of which has been coming more and more to light in the teaching of the church since the eighteenth century. It is actually to be found in the Bible itself, though not in so many words.

Bishop de Smedt believes (and I am sure that he is joined by the most thoughtful of the human race) that when the declaration on religious liberty is publicly proclaimed to the world, it will prove to be a definite contribution to civilized society.

As may be imagined, Bishop de Smedt was warmly applauded at the conclusion of his *relatio*. Joseph Conrad said years ago, "Give me the right word and right accent and I will move the world." The Bishop of Bruges seems to have both.

The second event of last week which rates a passing word in a diary of the council is the petition of 81 Catholic laymen from twelve nations asking the council fathers to set up a post-conciliar committee "to reconsider the present combination of pastoral duties with celibacy."

Nothing will be done about the question of celibacy at this council, of course, and this is not only because Pope Paul has asked that the question be eliminated from public debate but also because it is a relatively small group within the church that seems to be agitating it. The laymen of the petition, however, though small in number, are not without influence, and their numbers are likely to grow. They seem to believe in general that the unmarried state of priests is a handicap to their ministry and, in particular, that the shortage of priests in some parts of the world might be met if the obligation of celibacy, which is "not an intrinsic part of the evangelical mandate for the pastoral office," were removed.

As I look ahead into the future, I cannot but remember what

Fr. Tromp, author of one or two of the encyclicals of Pius XII, told a friend at the first session: "Pope John has opened a Pandora's box, but he does not know it"—and I am sure that Fr. Tromp is convinced that many of the troubles that will rise out of the opened box will be due to the new closer relationship with Protestant Christianity. I think that he is right; and it therefore behooves Protestant Christianity to order its life so that it will create as little disorganization in the sister church as possible. As for the three priestly vows, the Roman Catholic priest and the Protestant minister do not greatly differ on the matter of poverty. Neither one enters his profession in a spirit of gain. When it comes to celibacy and obedience, however, the influence of Protestant Christianity cannot but be combustive. How can it be anything else to those who believe that celibacy and implicit obedience are marks of the purity of the true church? We Protestants do not think they are, but our brothers do, and it is obvious that an exquisite sensitivity on our part in regard to these matters will be called for. I hope that future historians will recall that the so-called "crises" in these two areas were already developed before Vatican II opened the door to ecumenism. The new relationship with Protestant Christianity did not produce them, but I shall be surprised if eventually it does not set them on fire.

The debates did not come to an end with the recess, after all: discussion of the *schema* on "The Ministry and Life of Priests" was continued this morning, for fourteen fathers were ready to take the floor in the name of at least seventy others—though only seven of them had time to be heard before the noontime dismissal.

The very first intervention, by Bishop Arrieta Villalobos of Costa Rica, was on one of the very matters to which the petition had referred incidentally—not on celibacy (for the bishop made no mention of that) but on the shortage of priests in many parts of the world. "Shepherds in some places are dying without sheep," he said, "whereas in others, sheep are dying without shepherds." He asked that the maldistribution be met by the establishment of special seminaries for men dedicated to work in the sacerdotal disaster areas. He wanted a better recruiting system, and an elimination of curial restrictions on the transfer of certain categories of priests from one region to another. His plea was a fine mixture of reason and passion.

And two of the bishops spoke on obedience. Bishop Charbonneau of Hull, Canada, took what one might call a modern view of it: "A priest has his own pastoral grace, but he also shares in that of the bishop—and sharing means communion before it means dependence." Archbishop Connolly of Seattle stressed the implicit features I have alluded to. Obedience is, after all, obedience. "Even when a bishop is wrong, it is better for his priests to obey him. In the long run this will prove the better course for the church." "In our modern atmosphere, our priests have their own ideas as to how to run the diocese—a vice that goes with originality." "Our text should not be silent on this matter, lest it give the impression that obedience is less important today than it was yesterday."

Bishop DeRoo of Victoria, Canada, spoke of the priest as a man with a mission, a man on the march. His priesthood derives from the mission of the church, which in turn finds its own source in the mission of Christ. Bishop Flores Martin, of Spain, wanted the priesthood better defined in terms of the priesthood of the Bible; and Bishop Garcia Lahiguera, of the same country, appealing to his brother bishops to provide better spiritual direction for their priests, also proposed to the council that the church proclaim a new feast in honor of Christ the Eternal High Priest.

Music for the mass this morning was furnished by the boys' choir of Regensburg, popularly known as the "Cathedral Sparrows." But sparrows never sang as they did. They reminded me more of the hermit thrushes or the wood thrushes of our New Hampshire forests. "*Optime!*" said Archbishop Felici as he took the microphone immediately at the conclusion of their last hymn. He then went on to read a letter expressing the thanks of the Holy Father to Cardinal Liénart for his words of welcome on the return of His Holiness from his recent trip to the

United Nations. This also contained a blessing for all the bishops and a promise that the Pope's speech at the United Nations would be made a part of the council minutes.

☞ *Tuesday, October 26, 1965*

This morning mass was celebrated for us—or rather concelebrated—by four bishops and the Abbot General of the Cistercian Order. It was announced that the concelebration had been arranged to mark the close of the discussion of the *schema* dealing with priestly life and ministry, but the authorities that had planned the program in advance had counted their speeches before they were hatched—and the short morning was over before all of the scheduled interventions had been made. So the discussion will be closed tomorrow.

Yesterday the Secretary General had announced that the speeches of today on priestly life and ministry would be interspersed with votes on religious liberty. His words carried his characteristic humor: "Between balloting we shall have some consolation in listening to the fathers."

But actually there was little consolation to be found in the interventions, for the suggestions they contained had been heard by most of us lo! these countless times:

The dress of priests in any nation should be uniform, and of distinctive character.

The ministry of priests should be extended to the whole of life and not limited to the celebration of the sacrament.

The text should face the special difficulties created for priests in large, growing cities.

Priests should be encouraged to make a specialty of their work in the confessional—and not forget the importance of frequent confession on their own.

Mary, as the mother of the Eternal High Priest, is the mother of the priesthood.

Cooperation should be accorded those associations which are formed by diocesan priests to develop sanctity among them.

The *schema* should indicate the importance of intellectual activity in the life of the priest, even in secular fields—and his salary should be such as to enable him to surround himself with appropriate library and laboratory facilities. Amen.

At the close of the session, the results of the vote on the first paragraph of the *schema* on religious liberty were given out—2,031 for, 193 against. I dare say that a number of the negative ballots were cast by progressives who do not like the amendments now introduced "to make the *schema* conform to the Catholic faith." Emphasis is now placed on the obligation of all men to accept the Roman Catholic faith. Many feel that assertions of this sort belong to yesterday and are not in keeping with the contemporary ecumenical spirit. It is to be said, however, that the *schema* comes through with its assertion of the universal need for religious liberty uncompromised. In its field, therefore, the document is a landmark and should be hailed as such.

The discussion of priestly life and ministry at our afternoon meeting with the Secretariat was, I thought, livelier than that of the morning. Bishop Willebrands introduced Père Congar.

Père Congar started by reminding us that the present *schema* of thirty-two pages on the priesthood was the development out of a meager set of stiff and inadequate propositions first laid before the council and, as such, a vast improvement. He felt that it might go further, however, in setting forth what he called the "ontology" of the priesthood; that is, a studied answer to the question, What is a priest? He noted that the secularization of the world today had produced a crisis in the priesthood, many priests feeling a nagging sense of being somehow useless, or at least of being regarded as useless, in the community. Père Congar found too many priests immersed in work with practicing Roman Catholics, untouched by any purpose that led them beyond the walls of the church. Realizing that the *schema* could

not offer enough space for adequate discussion of priestly problems in today's detailed world, or for the subject of celibacy
(which, in a way, had been taken over by the Pope), he was
convinced that the document should say a great deal more about
the priesthood as a missionary vocation, cut loose from the cul-
tic priesthood of Aaron and redefined as the service of bringing
the gospel to all the people. "The consecration of the priest is a
consecration to mission, which includes but is not exhausted
by his offices at the altar."

Dr. Skydsgaard was the first to make an independent comment on the *schema*. He had culled out from it the sentences describing the life of a true priest—"He shares the perfection of
Christ," "he devotes himself completely to his people," and the
like—until it became clear that the hope expressed in the text
called for such an accumulation of virtues in a priest as today's
world had never seen and would never see. Dr. Skydsgaard
went on to point out that the bishops in council assembled might
well strike at once a more realistic and a more evangelical note
by saying to their priests quite simply and humbly, "Neither
you nor we can be perfect, but we can do our best, and Christ
can speak to our people even through our imperfections." Père
Congar told the Lutheran professor that he would make a good
Catholic bishop, and agreed that the document should be cast
in a far humbler mood. Bishop Willebrands also agreed that the
church should not come to its priests as a schoolmaster, but in
utmost sympathy with them should point them to the Holy Spirit.
Dr. Skydsgaard summed up the discussion by indicating that
the document in its present style stood in danger of becoming
law, which kills. "Arguments for sanctity can never take a legal
form."

Two men of Eastern churches, Frs. Nissiotis and Verghese
now made several points which seemed to characterize Orthodoxy.

The former argued that the priest at the altar cannot be said
so much to be ministering to the people as to be himself the
very personification of the people at the foot of the altar. He

does not have the right to say the liturgy by virtue of his ordination by a bishop: the whole church gives him that right—and he speaks therefore for the whole church and not for the hierarchy. (Père Congar thought this suggestion illuminating but felt that the whole priesthood could not be derived from the people. The priest is also a mediator of the things of God to the people. Returning to his own major point, he observed that if emphasis were put on the priesthood as a ministry, this would effect a synthesis between his service to the people and his identification with them.)

Fr. Verghese thought that the Aaronic priesthood is needed to interpret that of Christ himself—an idea that seemed to be supported by Père Congar, and also by Bishop Willebrands who later observed that the once-for-allness of Christ's sacrifice was oriented to the past as well as to the future.

Fr. Verghese defined the powers of priest and bishop as identical, save that the priest could not delegate his to others. "The Western word *potestas* should give way to the Eastern *charisma.*" Fr. Gregory Baum being called upon (Père Congar having had to leave) gave a Western definition of the distinction between the two offices: "The priest has the same grace as that enjoyed in its fullness by the bishop."

All through this little debate between Eastern and Western Catholicism on the difference between priest and bishop I felt the ghost of Dr. Freud hovering near. If the human mind is an inveterate rationalizer of its wishes, theology always runs the danger of becoming the cloak of sheer desire to adhere to tradition. Is either view tenable for a contemporary mind? Is it really true that a bishop, simply by virtue of his office, has more grace than a priest? And can he assign grace to another? Is a gift of the Infinite One so subject to a metric system? so susceptible to pickup and delivery? The conversations of the future will at least give us opportunity to reexamine these matters—but in the meantime, I am content to stay with Bishop Willebrands' sage observation and go no further into exacter definition. Said he, "There is unity as well as diversity between priest and bishop.

Both need each other; even the bishop cannot enjoy the grace that is given him without the priest." This is a truth that might well appear in the text of the *schema*.

Dr. Reid made several points. Père Congar's use of the phrase "prophet, priest, and king" would have pleased John Calvin. A priest's studies are not merely a means to an end. A priest's task is not merely to unite people to their bishops. The world should be recognized by the priest as the field from which he draws the forms of his life. Bishop Willebrands, hinting that the phrase "prophet, priest, and king" used of Christ, antedated Calvin, thought that the *schema* plays down the role of the priest as a prophet. "But it is chiefly in his prophetic function that a priest becomes part of his world—and priests will feel the lack of this emphasis in the promulgated document." The bishop has a knack of laying his finger on the real point at issue.

Fr. Baum, who now took over on the withdrawal of Bishop Willebrands, pointed out that consecration, narrowly understood, tends to separate the priest from the people, "making him a little chalice." He regarded the emphasis on the threefold office of Christ and his priests as a truer understanding of consecration and a definite sign of progress in the Roman church.

Fr. Thyssen asked if there were not some unifying conception of the priesthood which would synthesize the Eastern and Western ideas. He also asked the non-Romans for their idea of what a priest is. Mr. Lawrence, referring to the second question, indicated that the situation outside Rome is similar to that inside —that the clergy need to have their morale restored, not realizing how much the people really love them and depend upon them for saving truth.

Dr. Vischer pointed out that the historical statement in the *schema* as to the origin of bishops, priests, and deacons, is far too simple to fit the facts—and Fr. Baum promised to send this comment in to the council.

Fr. Davis, who is a student of Cardinal Newman, pointed out that the threefold ministry of Christ loomed large in the mind of Newman before he became a Roman Catholic, and that after his conversion he applied the idea to the whole church—one of his most fecund conceptions.

Dr. Faber, a Dutch Reformed churchman, representing the International Association of Religious Liberals, brought the discussion to an end by indicating that the image of the priest or minister, like that of almost every other leader in our changing society, is itself undergoing change. He asked that the problem be faced from a sociological as well as a theological angle.

☞ *Wednesday, October 27, 1965*

Yesterday was the final day of debate, after all. What happened to those bishops whose name appeared on yesterday's list as ready to speak will have to be left to some inquiring future historian. The Secretary General, as happy as the rest of us that the council now seems to be drawing to its close, bade us be content with not hearing speeches from now on: "In quietness and confidence shall be your strength." He congratulated the assembly that their labors were over and that they were now to garner the fruits.

Though the debate had been brought to an end, there was actually one more speech—by the Rt. Rev. Msgr. Thomas Falls, a pastor in Philadelphia, Pennsylvania. He spoke as a priest for the other priests of the world on the *schema* on the priesthood. I think the whole council was interested in what he had to say.

He praised the *schema* for making distinction between clergy and laity, for lifting into prominence the need for a common effort among diocesan clergy to develop the spiritual life, for maintaining at the center of the priestly life the celebration of daily mass, and for asking that fitting salaries be paid to priests. On the last point he thought that more concrete norms might have been laid down. With due respect to the married clergy of the Eastern Church, he approved what the *schema* had said, or not said, about celibacy.

Msgr. Falls thought that the text might have been more decisive on the nature of the priesthood. For himself, he believed that the ideal priest could be called a second Christ, participating in the sacrifice of Christ in all his work, and that though by its very nature his work was subordinate to that of the bishop, it partook of the same grace. Each priest has a particular responsibility to his own diocesan bishop.

He wanted the spirituality of the priest more carefully limned, as distinct from that of the religious and the laity, and he even outdid the text in celebrating the distinctive virtues of the priesthood—zeal, concern for all men, universal love, especially for children, the poor, and sinners, apostolic fervor and perseverance. It made a difference to have this homiletical bit from a priest himself, to hear a priest play up the priesthood.

The monsignor thought all priests should be devoted to Mary, the Mother of the Clergy, and concluded, followed by applause, with a pledge on behalf of all priests to help the bishops put the acts of the council into action.

From time to time in the course of the morning—the shortest business session on the records of the council, concluding shortly after eleven—votes on the *schema* on religious liberty were taken. There were 543 council fathers who refused to accept the first part of the *schema* as it is, but only an examination of the proposed amendments will reveal whether these votes came from disturbed conservatives or frustrated progressives.

Since tomorrow will be a day for promulgation, and next week a time of recess, every measure has been taken to keep the bishops here for the Friday session. Voting on the whole of the *schema* on revelation has been assigned to that day, and the bishops have not only been told that it is their duty to be present but today, hiding the ferrule and setting out the honey jar, Archbishop Felici stated that he hoped, without being absolutely certain, that on Friday it would be possible to distribute the medal commemorating the fourth session of the council.

📖 *Thursday, October 28, 1965*

The great public session of the council this morning started on time—at nine o'clock—and was over a few minutes after noon. This represents *aggiornamento* in itself, for the first sessions were far longer drawn out. Through the four years there has been a steady improvement in procedure. Again only two of the cardinals, representing the entire college, made their obeisance to the Holy Father, and only two of the patriarchs, archbishops, bishops, abbots, and superiors general. This kneeling before the Holy Father and kissing his ring is a completely un-Western and unmodern bit of symbolism, but it must be said of it that this morning it did not take much time. Time was also saved by putting the voting first, and then celebrating the mass, so that the ballots might be counted during the latter period and announced at the conclusion.

Observers and wives gathered at the Secretariat at eight o'clock. This year there were more of each than at any previous session. As the men, almost one hundred strong, marched in line, two by two, across the piazza of St. Peters, they were something of a *spectaculo* themselves, dressed in the vestments of their churches from all over the world. Our good Jesuit guide, Fr. Long, in a simple black cassock, seemed a veritable Puritan in comparison to some of the rest of us, especially those who brought with them the glad colors of their native India.

The wives as usual were conducted to good seats near the front in the south transept, and the observers sat, as we have sat before, in the rotunda just in front of the tribune of St. Longinus, which we occupy at business sessions.

We noticed that Cardinal Spellman had returned from New York.

Sitting next to Al Outler, I heard from him during the period of waiting for the events to begin that he has recently learned not a little about the very conservative and highly organized group, made up chiefly of Latins, who seem still determined to scotch the declaration on religious liberty if they can. Among the pamphlets that they have circulated is one quoting all that recent popes have said in their encyclicals on the subject of religious liberty—and, truth to tell, until one comes to John XXIII who, in *Pacem in Terris,* hints that a new wind is blowing, there seems to be hardly a vestige of support for the position taken in the new declaration, which will come up for penultimate vote after the council recess of next week.

There was no considerable negative vote, however, on any of the *schemata* brought forward for promulgation today. "The Bishops' Pastoral Office in the Church" could excite only two votes against it. "The Accommodated Renewal of the Religious Life," which is designed to bring the monastic orders up to date, found four dissenters. The *schema* on priestly training called out only three protests, the *schema* on Christian education only thirty-five.

It was feared that "The Relationship of the Church to Non-Christian Religions" (which included the famous section on the Jews) might reveal not a little dissent, but actually, in the final count, there were only eighty-eight who said no. This is due in part to the simple fact of timing. As I have noted before, the council fathers are now ready to go home—and an aye vote must in some cases be counted only a vote to get back to the diocese without any more continuance of controversy. Normally, I suppose the old lines represent some truth:

> All our fathers have been churchmen,
>   Nineteen hundred years or so,
> And to every new suggestion
>   They have always answered no.

Here the situation is now reversed:

> We've sat beneath St. Peter's dome
>   For four years more or less,
> And if it speeds our going home,
>   We'll gladly answer yes.

There had been some hope that the Pope, in his allocution, would give notice of the terminating day of the council—but no, his utterance proved to be a more general homily on the building of the church.

As I look back upon the morning session, I remember best the celestial singing of the choir, whose anthems filled the hall while the various ballots were being collected. The voices of the men and boys, superbly blended, mounted from the tenderest pianissimo into sheer majesty and power as the grand occasion at times demanded. The Roman church may not have given me my theology, but it has given me joys of music and beauty, as well as of friendship, which will console and strengthen me when I am no longer able to evaluate dogma.

✍ *Friday, October 29, 1965*

The mass this morning was in the Armenian rite. Like the Armenians themselves, the form of this mass, if one may judge by the music, has been oriented to the West and has advanced with the advancing generations. It is the first of the non-Latin masses we have heard this year, for instance, which has allowed modern harmony in the Western scale to displace the henophony of the ancient chants—and the result gives an impression of vigor. Especially beautiful was the Sanctus, sung in four parts, meaning and mode well married to each other.

At the outset of the business session, the Secretary General announced that the medals struck to commemorate the fourth session of the council would be distributed at eleven. This is the critical hour when a large portion of the morning population of St. Peters drifts away to the coffee bars. The medals would be rewards of merit for staying in one's seat and voting as a proper council father should.

Actually, the number of council fathers present, though slightly diminished, was greater than might have been expected on the day before a long recess.

Though the business of the morning was to vote on the various amendments to the *schema* on divine revelation, in the intervals between the balloting, the Russian choir of St. John of Damascus, from Essen, Germany, a group of perhaps seventy-five men and women who are giving concerts elsewhere in the city today and tomorrow, sang songs of Slavic Orthodoxy with great effect. Our Dr. Grotoff, one of the observers, himself a Russian, found several friends among them.

The voting was introduced by Cardinal Florit and Bishop Charue, the latter reading the *relatio* for Bishop van Dodewaard. Cardinal Florit dwelt at some length on a particular amendment submitted by several fathers, which had nonetheless been rejected by the commission. These fathers had asked that the text speak not of the progress of tradition, but only of progress in the understanding of tradition. This was rejected for the interesting and, as I believe, sound reason that tradition, as something living, transmitted from generation to generation, while not changing in substance, does actually grow. Truth and tradition are not quite the same thing. (The Pilgrims' minister John Robinson remarked that our Lord never said, "I am the tradition.")

One accepted amendment is to the effect that the church does not acquire her certainty about revealed truth solely through the Bible. Any modern Protestant would, I think, agree to this, even though some of his ancestors raised the slogan "*sola Scriptura.*" The average Protestant, however, probably differs from the average Roman Catholic in his belief that it is the internal witness of the Holy Spirit in himself, rather than the authority of the church, which guarantees the truth he finds in the Bible. I imagine that in future dialogue it will be discovered that these two positions may be merged in the idea that the very authority of the church lies in the witness of the Holy Spirit which comes to its members.

Late in the afternoon, at the informal meeting of the English-speaking observers with Frs. Norris and O'Hanlon, we took up the same question, starting off with a question by Mr. Cuttriss of Australia as to the actual definition of *what it is that is transmitted in tradition.* We all agreed with Fr. Norris that the *schema* had celebrated a notable triumph in moving away from the idea of tradition as a series of theological propositions and to the truth that what moves from generation to generation and holds the church together is the living Holy Spirit who is sent by Christ himself.

The results of the final votes on the amendments to the *schema* on religious liberty were given this morning. The largest number of *ayes with reservations* (which, as I have indicated before, have the same effect as *noes with reservations*) was 417, as against Wednesday's 543. Neither of these is large enough to wreck the structure of the *schema,* for even without them the text receives more than the required two-thirds majority; but all the amendments will be carefully considered and the usual vote upon them taken later. Many of the proposed amendments will be found to be identical, for the organized company of conservatives, popularly known as "Carli and Company" have prepared *modi* and distributed them among friends to turn in. This is of course wholly legitimate, and not unlikely to produce results—and it therefore still leaves us wondering whether the good ship Religious Liberty has yet reached the open sea, out of danger of hidden reefs. I saw Fr. John Courtney Murray in the hospital on Wednesday, where he has been for the last two or three weeks. God grant he may be present in a fortnight or so, when the *schema* on religious liberty will come up for final and, we pray, victorious vote. Out of his mind and spirit have come the warp and woof of it.

The Secretary General did not this morning tell us when the council would end, but such announcements as he made indicate that the best guess is still December 8. After another public session on November 18, there arises the probability of a third longish recess.

The council, to all intents and purposes, is about over. The atmosphere of last things prevails.

THE SEVENTH WEEK
[NOVEMBER 9-13]

📖 *Tuesday, November 9, 1965*

General congregations were renewed today, after a recess of ten days, in the course of which Mildred and I had a most satisfactory visit to the Taizé community in France, driving there and back in a car lent to us in unstinted generosity by Lydia Englebert.

The morning began with a mass celebrated in the Byzantine-Melchite rite. The first anthems were unusual, a single melody being carried by the higher voices while the basses maintained a somber but musical monotone far below. At times the cantor picked up the last note of the celebrant's chant an octave below. For the most part the music was Western, polyphonic, and spiritually searching.

The rite lasted for well over an hour, however, and in its forms was about as remote from anything we see today in the West as the rising is from the setting sun. The more I witness these ornate ceremonies, bedizened with the splendors of the past, the deeper chiseled my prejudice against them seems to be. I like them; I think they are fun; but as vehicles of worship they seem thin and unreal for the simple reason that there is no bridge between them and the ordinary life I lead with God and my fellowmen. Perversely I am glad that someone main-

131

tains them and hope that they will continue to do so, but with reduced frequency. It is one thing to visit a museum of antiquities now and then, and another thing to live there.

The results of the voting on "Divine Revelation" before the recess were announced this morning—all overwhelmingly affirmative.

This morning the voting was on "The Apostolate of the Laity." Some last minute changes were offered, but none of them disturbing to the substance of the document. The most important was the introduction of a sentence calling for youth to witness to Christ. In his introduction to this final edition of the *schema*, Bishop Hengsbach mentioned the request that the title of it be changed from "The Apostolate of the Laity" to "The Participation of the Laity in the Mission of the Church." The latter would have accorded more with common usage today, and would certainly have been better understood by Protestants, but it had been decided by the commission finally to keep to the time-honored phraseology of the Roman Catholic Church. In chapter 3 important interpolations have been made calling for a broader participation by women in the church's apostolate. The text has peculiar significance, being the first put out by any Catholic council dealing specifically with the apostolate of the laity. The votes of approval, taken in the course of the morning, were all of them almost unanimous.

Before the recent recess began, the bishops had been told that they would receive copies of a draft statement prepared by the Sacred Penitentiary, the committee of the curia which deals with indulgences. The various national conferences of bishops were asked to meet in the course of the week to discuss this declaration and, if desired, report their opinion about it. This was a document of ninety pages which, we are now told, did not reach the hands of most of the bishops until the very day it was to be discussed, and in some cases not until the very day on which the results of the discussion were to be announced.

Since Martin Luther's protest against abuses in indulgences is usually considered the spark that set off the conflagration of the Reformation, we Protestants pricked up our ears at mention of the discussion—though of course we had no part, not even that of observers, in the meetings of the episcopal conferences.

The story of the sudden emergence of this theme among the council fathers (advisedly put this way, since it is not a theme of the council itself) seems to begin with the request of certain bishops, notably those of Aberdeen and Chiusi, during the days of preparation for the council, that the subject be actually taken up on the floor of St. Peters. This request was turned down by the authorities. Thereupon the Sacred Penitentiary, consisting chiefly of church lawyers of the old school, saw an opportunity to make such changes in the regulations and procedures as it deemed necessary, all within the framework of current canon law, without benefit of or annoyance from the council. So they put out their document of "reform"; and it seems that it was Pope Paul himself, urged by many who thought the proposed changes pitifully inadequate, who decided last summer that the draft proposal should be laid before the bishops' conferences.

Indulgences have a long history. In the early centuries of the church, a sinner was reconciled to the church only after a period of penance, being supported in his course of repentance by the prayers of the local Christian community. About a thousand years ago a system began to take form whereby the periods of penance imposed by the church could be shortened by "indulgences." These indulgences were supposedly the fruit of the prayers of the church for the sinner. These prayers were regarded as being available from "the treasury of the church."

It is easy to see how abuses could enter into such a system, especially after the ancient penitential discipline of the church had died out. In especial, people began thinking of any given number of days indulgence as meaning that number of days less in purgatory. It made for an impersonal, metered piety, quite foreign to the idea that God forgives sin out of his own sheer grace and not because of any particular merit of the repentant sinner. So now the Sacred Penitentiary was ready to reform the code. We in the observers' seats—all of us, since the

system of indulgences has the same short shrift in Eastern Orthodoxy as it does in Protestant Christianity—were agog to know
how this would be done.

And this morning Cardinal Cento and *Peritus* Sessolo, chairman and secretary of the Penitentiary, told us how.

The numerical counting of indulgences is to be discontinued.
A partial indulgence attached to a prayer or pious work will be
designated simply as a "partial indulgence" without any de-
termination of days or years. "Through such an indulgence, ecclesiastical authority grants to a member of the church, from
the treasury of the church, as much remission before God of the
temporal punishment due to sin as he has already acquired
through the prayer of pious work." This is the proposal that the
young and irreverent seminarians in Rome are said to call
"matching funds."

Again, the number of indulgences granted is to be reduced.
A "plenary indulgence" originally canceled all of the ecclesiastical penance imposed for a sin and today is equivalent to complete forgiveness of it: the plan is to reduce these to no more
than one a day for any one person. "One a day": it has not taken
the American seminarians long, in view of the name of a well
advertised medicament, to dub this the vitamin system.

The custom has grown up of applying a special plenary indulgence to a particular soul in purgatory through the celebration
of a mass. This custom, or at least this description of what takes
place, is to be abolished, since the fruits of the celebration of
a mass are in principle infinite, being in the hands of God, and
they cannot be particularized by man.

As a matter of fact, it is more than young seminarians that
regard the system of indulgences with skepticism. In English-
speaking countries the attitude of church leaders to it seems to
be complete indifference. When our translators this morning were
giving us the English for the *relator's* Latin, it cannot be said
that they did not flavor their translation with their personal feelings. When the *relator* was speaking about "the treasury of the
church," he apparently lost his place; a long silence ensued dur-

ing which the interpreter remarked *sotto voce*, "They're looking for that treasury."

We shall hear more of this. It may be that tomorrow morning the bishops themselves will speak out, for the various conferences will be permitted to make public their reports at that time, if they care to.

At the end of the morning the council sat for some time quietly awaiting a distribution of the next *schema*—but it finally got so late that they were dismissed *schema*-less.

They all went home, however, with a firmer step than has been usual recently—for today the great announcement was made: the council will be brought to an end on December 8, the Feast of the Immaculate Conception.

This afternoon the observers gathered to discuss with the Secretariat the new "ecumenical directory" which the Secretariat is busily engaged in preparing. This will go out first in somewhat tentative form; and later a more permanent document will be prepared on the basis of the reaction to the first one. It will take up organization, the meaning of baptism, common worship, dialogue, education, all with a view to using these for the promotion of Christian unity.

Fr. John Long presided this afternoon, in place of Bishop Willebrands, the latter being engaged, with many other members of the Secretariat, in disposing of the last of the 3,500 amendments to the *schema* on religious liberty.

At the meeting last week, which I did not attend, since it was held during the recess, they began the discussion of the directory. There the need was stressed for the ecumenical education of laymen, and not simply seminarians. It was suggested that the Secretariat might be decentralized, so that members of it would be available in places other than Rome. Perhaps the most important suggestion was that in the formation of diocesan commissions on unity, it is well from the very outset to consult non-Roman Christian leaders.

Today the talk touched many points. I reported on our happy experience in New Hampshire where, on the Roman Catholic

commission, there sit not only priests but also laity in both kinds
and, *mirabile dictu,* four non-Romans with voice but no vote.
Several thought that the ecumenical work already existing in the
world, and in a state of some maturity, might well be mentioned
in the directory. Professor Schlink and Mr. Lawrence, both per-
plexed if not shocked by the statement on indulgences, asked if
that might be discussed by the observers. Fr. Long felt that it
should, and "on its own merits," said he, "if we can use that
term." I have yet to talk face-to-face with a Roman Catholic who
has anything good to say about the present or the proposed system of indulgences.

The afternoon was closed with one of Fr. Borovoy's pleasant
explosions. He always contrives to communicate his emotions,
and without ill effect. His straightforwardness melts resentment.
In Russian, being interpreted in French, he made it quite clear
that he did not like the way in which Rome sometimes treated
Orthodox baptisms. "Why, there is greater discrimination against
us than there is against the Jews!" Nor does he like Roman ana-
themas, Roman indulgences, or the Roman attitude in mixed
marriages. It would take a long directory to describe the changes
that Fr. Borovoy would like to see in the Church of Rome—and
it might appropriately be named Suggestions Looking Toward
Utopia.

📖 *Wednesday, November 10, 1965*

Two colleague-observers of mine of the International Congregational Council are here at the moment—Ruben Huenemann
(and his wife), who has just come, and Edgar Chandler, who
does not go until the end of this week.

Harold Wilke was a visitor at the general congregation this
morning, and so was the Pope, the former just passing through

the city, the latter staying for a longer time. The Vatican choir of men and boys was on hand for the mass, also, filling the great basilica with loveliness beyond expression. I noticed that the news release says that as His Holiness left, after the mass, he greeted "with a special gesture, the non-Catholic observers, as he passed before their tribune." His courtesy is never-failing.

In opening the business period, Archbishop Felici gave a word of praise to the ushers, who constantly pass up and down the tribunes of the bishops, serving their needs, which are many and sundry. The ushers' beneficiaries warmly applauded.

Applause also greeted the announcement that the *schema* on "The Apostolate of the Laity," thanks to the overwhelmingly affirmative votes taken yesterday at the close of the session, is now ready for the Pope to sign, seal, and deliver to the world.

The Very Rev. John Schütte, Superior General of the Society of the Divine Word and Vice President of the council's Commission on Missions, submitted the revised *schema* on missionary activity. The amendments to the draft previously submitted had filled 550 printed pages, all of which had been read and as far as possible incorporated into the text.

The new text seems a vast improvement on the old. It urges the necessity of missions far more strongly than the other. Though it still clings to the idea that the mandate of Christ, "Go into all the world," was directed chiefly to the apostles, and therefore to the bishops, an effort has been made to balance this by stressing the missionary vocation of all the people of God. It calls upon the newly founded churches to become missionary churches —*missionatae* or sending churches, rather than merely *missionariae* or receiving churches—as soon as possible. Though it does not invite particular dioceses to take over particular mission territories, as was suggested by some, it does not close the door to the possibility. And instead of constituting the Sacred Congregation for the Propagation of the Faith from "representatives of all the national episcopal conferences," it leaves the matter of representation to the Pope.

To us observers the text is magnificently improved by the

new references to ecumenism. The *schema* now speaks of the
divisions of Christianity as "obscuring the message of peace and
closing the door of faith to many." It recommends collaboration
"not only among individual Christians but among churches as
such." It recommends that the Congregation for the Propagation
of the Faith "together with the Secretariat for Christian Unity
seek ways and means for securing fraternal collaboration and
organized common life with the missionary undertakings of other
Christian communions, that the scandal of division may be done
away."

The new-dawn quality of these references is more fully conceived when the notes upon them are read, for it is plainly stated
there that one or two of them come as a direct result of suggestions made by the observers. I believe that this is the first time
in history that an official Roman Catholic document has made
any such declaration as this. The *relator* expressed the hope that
his Christian brothers would respond positively, even warmly, to
these invitations to cooperation. Any one who would not must
certainly be deaf to what the Spirit is saying to the churches.

The first of the presidents of the national episcopal conferences
to present his report on the paper on indulgences was the Patriarch Maximos IV Saigh, who commanded silence from his first
word, as he always does. There is no one in the council, I think,
who has hit the nail on the head more strongly or more con-
sistently than he. Speaking for the Greek Melchite bishops, he
declared the power of the church to add to the merit of a good
act through its intercession "but," said he, "to equate remission
by the church with the forgiveness of God has caused irreparable
harm to the church. For eleven centuries there was no trace of
indulgences in the church, even in the West. Indulgences are
linked with the ancient penitential discipline of the church."
Here, in his written speech, as appears in the news release, he
went on to say, "and the disappearance of this discipline should
also have entailed the disappearance of indulgences." Actually,
however, he did not quite say that: someone, fearing too great
an explosion, had apparently asked him to leave it out. But he

went on, in language almost as strong. "The church should work the whole system over. This means suppressing any question of days and years." This the draft does. "It means that we must get rid of the arithmetic idea." This the draft does not do, since the "matching funds" concept is pure arithmetic. "We must eliminate the thought that indulgences have an automatic effect, apart from the spiritual effort of the person." This the draft at least attempts. "The emphasis must be placed on the spirit of the individual. This will obviate doctrinal difficulties with the churches of the Reformation, disciplinary difficulties with those of the East, and pastoral difficulties with Catholics themselves." One had the feeling that Maximos was minimizing his own feelings, and that if he had really let his convictions be fully known, he would have put the whole system in Tophet.

Others reported, but in general simply gave the votes of their bishops on the several particular questions asked: "Do you approve what we have done about partial indulgences? plenary indulgences?" etc. There was general approval.

This was true even of the American bishops, though from Cardinal Shehan's report it was evident that a saving remnant realizes that the draft takes no account of recent developments in Roman Catholic thought. I judged it was his own idea that the whole matter should be placed in the hands of competent theologians within each episcopal conference and reported on after careful examination. There are certainly some who would like to let this sleeping dog lie, in the expectation that he will eventually die in his sleep. The priests I have talked with wish with Maximos that all indulgences had gone out with the old penitential system.

There is an auditor in an invalid chair who is often wheeled to the altar by one of his fellows to take communion at the mass which opens the general congregation. This morning there were a number of people in wheel chairs, a pilgrimage of the sick, I believe, who received communion not at the main altar but at their places in the visitors' enclosure, and with wafers brought not from the main altar but from the reserved sacrament in the south transept at which visitors communicate at the same time as, and as part of, the main celebration. It is a sign of the church's strength that it does not lose its compassion for the weak.

Archbishop Felici made one or two little speeches this morning about the nomenclature of the council, distinguishing between "congregations" and "sessions" and recalling the number of each which had been held—a performance which, in the Latinity of this council, can only be called *temporicide*—killing time. In order to give opportunity to the commissions to finish their work, the time of the council during these last days simply has to be strung out, if not strung up.

"Petering out at St. Peters" might well have been the title given to these last days, had it not been for the sudden appearance of the exciting item of indulgences. We do not have any Martin Luther here to nail his protests to the cathedral door, but we do have plenty of people to nail their protests anywhere that people will read them.

This morning we heard Cardinal Wyszynski, speaking for the bishops of Poland, Cardinal de Arriba y Castro, for those of Spain, and Cardinal Urbani, for Italy, who in general approved the draft of the Penitentiary. They thought that it ought to be brought into harmony with other documents of Vatican II, that it might present clearer definitions of such misunderstood matters as plenary indulgence, and that, in especial, it should contain in an introduction a theology of indulgences in epitome. But on the whole, they seemed to stand with the Penitentiary.

But northwestern Europe also spoke. My current impression, like my earlier ones, is that this is the brain-center of the church.

It began with Cardinal Alfrink of the Netherlands, speaking for all the bishops of his conference. Dispassionate but devastating, he pointed to the basic disharmony between the practice of indulgences and the best current theology about them. "The text at hand does not eliminate this disagreement." Showing that the idea of vindictive punishment still lingered in the lines of the document, the kind of punishment from which the church is supposed to free the faithful, he called for a thorough revision in the light of current theological research.

Later, and conclusively, Cardinals König, Archbishop of Vienna, and Döpfner, Archbishop of Munich, entered the field, each of them speaking for the bishops of both Austria and Germany. Cardinal König at first threw out a few bits of praise for the document to attract his opponents out of their defenses. "The bishops are pleased that a complete revision of indulgences has been undertaken." But then he began to swing his mace. "The present practice of indulgences reduces the relation of man to God to a mathematical level. It is full of misunderstandings. And the present document does not help: it is not sufficiently mature in its thinking, since it pays no attention to present-day theological thought. It is guilty of a careless use of the sacred scripture. It blandly presents controverted matters of great doubt as if they were generally accepted. Who is willing to define invisible temporal punishment, for instance, as it is seen by the eyes of God? Dogmatic, ecumenical, and scriptural considerations call for a complete recasting of the text."

This cut a swath for Cardinal Döpfner's deadly military engine. Going back into history, the latter conceded that visible indulgences were rational enough when they were used to reduce visible penances, but when they came to be applied to invisible penances, their irrationality invited superstition. The expression "treasury of the church" is to be understood as an analogy: the

treasury of the church is God himself, who supports the efforts
of any man against sin, through Christ. "The presentation of indulgences in our text is entirely too individualistic, whereas an
indulgence consists essentially in the intervention of the church
and takes the shape of the church's prayer for the sinner." He
wound up his succinct but powerful presentation of contemporary
thought on indulgences with three recommendations. 1. The document should not be promulgated at this time. 2. The work of
revision should be entrusted to a commission with a broadened
membership, including an adequate number of trained theologians. 3. After adequate study by such a commission, a papal
document should be prepared with directives to meet the needs
of these times.

Cardinal Alfrink had spoken quietly, allowing the truth of
what he said to make its own appeal. Cardinal König had warmed
to the subject, pouring in not a little Teutonic eagerness. Cardinal
Döpfner threw himself wholly into his presentation. It was not
strange that the council burst into applause when he closed.

I think the American bishops feel that they missed a trick in
simply reporting the number of their votes on the various specific
questions. Many of them being booked for excursions out of
Rome, some of them for quick trips back home, they held no
meeting, and depended simply upon written replies to a question-
naire. Cardinal Shehan did the best he could under the circumstances, but his report did not begin to influence the assembly
like that of yesterday from Maximos IV, and those of today from
the Dutch and German-speaking leaders.

As the annual sessions of the council have drawn toward their
last days, there has always been an increase in social engagements. This final session is proving no exception. Today, for instance, there were no less than three extracurricular meetings,
all important. For luncheon I went with other men interested in
education to the Gregorian University, where we were guests
of the faculty at the long tables of their refectory. I sat next to
Fr. Witte, whom I had already met several times and who is ex-
pecting to visit the United States this summer. At 4:30 we went

to the annual reception given by the Paulist Fathers to the American hierarchy and the English-speaking observers, and there Dr. Outler gave a superb address on "Reformation—Roman Style." Thereafter we stopped in at a reception given by Canon and Mrs. Findlow, Canon Findlow being the representative of the Archbishop of Canterbury here at the seat of the Church of Rome.

ᗡ *Friday, November 12, 1965*

The mass this morning was celebrated in memory of St. Josaphat, the martyr, who, as I have mentioned before in this diary, was an ardent missionary for Rome among the Orthodox groups of the Ukraine 350 years ago, being finally assassinated by his enemies. There is every reason to hail him as a martyr of the faith, but to appoint him a patron of the movement toward unity between the Eastern and Western churches is surely the result of a blind spot on the Roman retina for the simple reason that, though he is a forerunner of ecumenicity to Rome, the Orthodox regard him as an arrant proselytizer. It is a little like asking the Roman church to regard Martin Luther as an influence for unity —for he did, after all, believe in church unity in his own style.

The music of the Ukrainian mass, sung by the students of the Pontifical Ukrainian College of St. Josaphat, dispelled all thought of the difficulties surrounding their patron saint. From the first note we knew that it was going to be vigorous and genuine. Now there were daring but successful harmonies, now not a little of Russian abandon in their melodies. The cherubic hymn needs sopranos to reach its perfection, but in other anthems the mighty basses carried all before them.

The Great Entrance of the Eastern rites, when the communion elements are brought in, in procession, is always effective. The

communion was in both kinds, wafers of lozenge size being
poured into the wine and, so saturated, placed with a spoon,
one by one, on the tongue of each communicant.

It was a leisurely service. "Seventy minutes," I murmured to
Douglas Steere as I passed to another seat. "Seventy-one," he
returned in the same tone. Improving on the Prayer Book, we
had each apparently been so passing through things eternal that
we had lost not the things temporal.

Someone secured for us this morning mimeographed copies of
Cardinal Döpfner's stirring speech of yesterday. Either because
the revolutionary explosion of that session had caused the program makers to alter their plans for this morning or because there
was actually no time for anything but voting, there were no
speeches about indulgences today.

Announcement was made this morning of the votes taken yesterday on the *schema* on "The Missionary Activity of the Church,"
and to my surprise, there were over 700 votes "with reservations"
against chapter 5. The statement that seems to stick in the crop
of the council is judged by most to be that which, while asking
that the commission on missions at Rome be made up of bishops
from the whole world, and others, leaves the "ways and means"
of appointing them to the Roman Pontiff—which means his curia.
The bishops want a more definite directive than this, which will
be less open to usurpation by conservative Rome. The large
negative vote means that the document will now doubtless be
laid on the desk of the Pope—which is exactly where the negative voters want to see it. We may be hearing more about this
in the next, and final, edition of the text.

Lectures by Karl Rahner, Yves Congar, and other progressives
have been scheduled in a hall not far from St. Peters for the
month of November. The Secretary General this morning said
that he had been asked whether these lectures were to be regarded as official or at least as authorized. He answered with a
good, round, unequivocal NO. Middle-of-the-road men such as
he do not yet feel at home with the trailblazers.

When, a moment ago, I was speaking of the speeches on in-

dulgences, I should have noted that *L'Osservatore Romano* has
let it be known only that such speeches had been given. It has
not described their content. This curial house organ apparently
desires to give the impression that the statement on indulgences
produced by the Penitentiary is receiving the general approval
of the council. Cardinal Döpfner's stinging commentary was not
commented upon.

This morning Archbishop Marty presented the revised *schema*
on "The Ministry and Life of Priests." This is a good, but not
a brilliant piece of work. To those of us who have known the
ministry, it seems to have more than its share of pious generaliza-
tion. "In the midst of preaching, conducting worship, and govern-
ing the faithful" (the Roman way of saying "running the church"),
"the priest should not forget those outside the church." This is
a fair sample of the keenness of its cutting edge.

If the morning for the most part was not devoted to the killing of time, it was at least designed to exhaust it, for after the
amended *schema* on priestly life and ministry was introduced,
the first half of it was read, word for word. Here Rome did what
we Protestants always do when the church lawyers get hold of
our assemblies—as if printing had not been invented and reading was an art still known only to the few. The secretaries took
turns reading the text aloud, during which the fathers variously
dozed, chatted, read their mail, sipped coffee in the bar, sat and
read their breviaries, or simply sat.

This afternoon the English-speaking contingent of the Secretariat and the observers had a good two-hour conversation on
the subject of revelation, under the expert theological leadership
of Fr. Barnabas Ahern of the Passionist Fathers and Fr. Francis
McCool, S.J. We plan to repeat these encounters fairly frequently
in the near future, for we have come to know each other so well
that we have no fear of taking up subjects on which there is
Catholic-Protestant sensitivity and no hesitation at getting quickly
to the nub of the problem.

When I came into the basilica this morning, I found workmen laying down a heavy wooden ramp on the broad steps in front of the entrance; and on the inside I found they had prepared the chapel, whence Michelangelo's Pietà had been taken, for its return from the World's Fair in New York.

Once again, there were no reports from the bishops' conferences on indulgences, and in the course of the morning we were told that because of the priority of the voting, there would no longer be time for any more. The gossip is that the Canadian intervention, written largely by Fr. Gregory Baum under the eye of Cardinal Léger and other progressive leaders was so completely withering to the whole practice that conservative authorities had asked that it be turned in without being read aloud to the council, and that this procedure had now been adopted for all of the reports. Certain it is that the Secretary General, in asking for presidents of the episcopal conferences to submit their reports in writing, also asked them to bear in mind that they had been asked not to undertake a theological study of the question but only to answer a few simple questions on the revision of the existing discipline. But the fat is now in the fire, the flames are mounting up, the controversy is now burning, and its warmth will not be reduced until basic questions about indulgences have been asked and modernly answered.

The Secretary General told us that some had complained that he joked too much about solemn matters. To this he replied with characteristic whimsy, "In general from this rostrum I must merely repeat what others have told me to say: I do not like to give up my jokes, for it is only over them that I have any authority." And may he be protected in this authority to the last moment of the council, especially during these barren days of text-reading. One does not need to accept his conservatism and his sometimes autocratic ways of handling opponents to count him an unusually gifted master of ceremonies.

Reading, reading, reading—it consumed virtually the whole morning, until early dismissal, shortly before 11:30, allowed the fathers who wished to do so to get off in good time for the Dante celebration in Florence.

THE EIGHTH WEEK
[NOVEMBER 15-19]

✒ *Monday, November 15, 1965*

When I came in this morning, the Pietà was in place, but the chapel where it stands was all boarded up, so that one had to look at it through the cracks between the boards—and there were plenty of bishops doing so.

This morning there was not even mention of indulgences. By the speech of Cardinal Döpfner, who was the last to comment, we may say that a complete cycle has been rounded out. In a St. Peters built by indulgences, in the presence of Protestants whose fathers, under the leadership of a monk from Germany, broke with Rome as a reaction to indulgences, a cardinal from Germany has brought to an end the discussion of indulgences by pointing like Luther to the potential evils of indulgences.

Announcement was made this morning of the final votes on "The Ministry and Life of Priests." An unusual number of amendments were offered on the last two articles of the last chapter— 630 on the second, and 544 on the third. These probably cover a number of different points, however, and will constitute no impediment to passage.

Schema 13, dealing with "The Church in the Modern World," was introduced this morning by Archbishop Garrone of Toulouse, for voting. It is a notable improvement over the previous

149

edition. The three issues that had claimed the special attention of the council—atheism, marriage, war and peace—are far more decisively dealt with. The paragraphs on atheism have been given welcome sophistication by the Secretariat for Non-Christians, presided over by Cardinal König. Throughout the document, the exaggerated optimism of the former text has been toned down by more somber and realistic references to human sin, but the hope of the Christian gospel has likewise been emphasized, so that the *schema* is now more like life itself—a canvas of various shades of grey, through which filters a light that never was on sea or land.

Bishop McGrath of Santiago Veraguas of Panama, read a companion introduction to the expository premise. He pointed out that in this part, as in the entire *schema,* the commission had made a serious attempt to make the text more universal—so that it would be applicable to more than the Western world—and less deterministic—so as to recall to men their power of influencing their own situation in history.

Once more, in one of the notes, there is a reference to improvement suggested by observers.

At 4:15 this afternoon the English-speaking groups of observers met with Frs. Norris and O'Hanlon and other theologians whom they had invited to be present, to discuss the whole matter of worship. As usual, the debate proved lively and fruitful.

➩ *Tuesday, November 16, 1965*

The Vienna Boys' Choir provided a lovely framework of song for the mass this morning.

The first item on the business docket was the announcement of the votes taken yesterday. The largest number of amendments on any one chapter were those on chapter 3, "Human Activity in the World." Given the variety of subjects treated in the chapter, it is not surprising that this total ran so high. It does not endanger the future of the *schema*.

When the voting on the first part of *schema* 13, "The Church in the Modern World," was completed, Bishop Hengsbach of Essen introduced Part II. This throws the searchlight of the church on the problems of family, human culture, socio-economic life, political community, and peace and war. It is the first and last of these subjects that presented the greatest challenge. In no sense is the document one of pontification: the bishop closed with a plea to all to help the commission better this already greatly improved text.

We were glad to hear that laymen had cooperated on all the sub-commissions and particularly that the special papal commission had cooperated in drawing up the section on marriage and the family. The *schema* says a good deal on this subject, but does not invade the territory reserved for the special commission—the report from which the church can hardly wait to hear. The section being voted upon here attempts to find a middle path that touches on the one hand upon the primacy of conjugal love and, on the other, on the demands of the whole moral order and the teaching of the church. It leaves to the choice of parents the number of children that they shall have but furnishes norms on the basis of which the choice may be made. So the question of birth control is still open in the Roman church.

But the question is far from being what it was before the council began. Then considered by many to be closed by decision of the church, it is now open to all the winds of controversy. The very appointment of a commission to study it defines it as unsettled. From all over the world the Pope is now receiving petitions from international and other groups begging him to act in the way they conceive to be for the greatest good of humanity. A vast company within the church takes one side, an equally impressive company the other. Such circumstances would seem to argue that the Holy Father will come to his decision about it with the greatest deliberation, hoping that some consensus will have taken shape out of the present confusion.

The other subject on which a great many suggestions for improvement had been offered is that of war and peace. Here the commission found itself weighed down by the same perplexity that robs Christian political leaders of their sleep—how to reconcile the obligation of self-defense with that of avoiding fratricidal war. The text praises nonviolence, condemns such crimes as genocide and blind obedience to criminal military orders, denounces total war and the plague of the race for armaments, and hails the establishment of an international public authority (though it does not mention by name the United Nations).

Two additions to the text on the chapter on culture are worthy of note, each for its own reason. The place of women in cultural life is recognized and given new emphasis. And, in the second place, the words of Pope John XXIII, spoken in his original allocution to the council four years ago—describing the distinction between eternal truth, which remains unchanged from age to age, and the expression of that truth which must be adapted to the thought-forms of any given age—words which I have long since regarded as epitomizing the whole philosophy of *aggiornamento*—are introduced verbatim into the text. This has special meaning for progressive Roman theologians, for the utterance of Pope Paul VI in his encyclical *Mysterium fidei*, published just before this session of the council, has by some been taken as a declaration that certain expressions of truth must remain unchanged from age to age. The new statement will help to play down this interpretation of the papal utterance.

Here lies a nuance of difference between Roman and Protestant thinkers. For the latter, there is no contemporary spokesman to whose thought they try to adjust their own ideas.

In the chapters on socio-economic life and political community, there are no shattering changes in the new text.

At the end of the morning, after we had listened, or at least been exposed, to the oral reading of the endless paragraphs to be voted upon, the Secretary General brought the session to an end in his best style with a quotation from Virgil, *Sat prata biberant*—the fields have drunk enough—of battle.

At the meeting with the Secretariat this afternoon, Archpriest Kniazeff of the Orthodox Theological Institute of St. Serge of Paris, gave a eulogy on his predecessor, Bishop Cassian, who died early this year. He was an old friend of mine and of many. We shall all miss his quiet benevolence.

The subject of discussion was indulgences. Fr. Gregory Baum started us off with an outline of current Catholic thought on the subject. He regards indulgences as the healing prayers of the church applied to sinners. Though the old theology is no longer tenable, he sees in the system two basic values which should be saved—the idea that no Christian lives alone, without the help of the church, and the further idea that reconciliation to God, after his forgiveness, is a complex affair which calls for special pastoral care by the church.

The non-Romans present were most self-restrained. They had actually asked for this discussion on reading the draft put out by the Penitentiary, but now that Cardinal Döpfner and others had spoken, revealing a concern for a change in indulgence practices within the church, they were not inclined to repeat the defiant arguments of the Protestant Reformation again, lest in any way they should jeopardize the good fight being fought within Rome itself. Paul Verghese and others made thoughtful contributions to the debate, which Bishop Willebrands, who was presiding, afterward asked for in writing, in order that he might place them in the proper Roman hands.

When I asked about the present position of the *positio* or draft by the Penitentiary, Fr. Baum replied that he thought the lethal aim of Patriarch Maximos, and Cardinals Alfrink, König, and Döpfner had shot it down. In the providence of God, however, it had done a salutary work, for it had brought into the public arena a subject that will now be taken up and carried to completion by the theologians. The unpublished interventions of Canada, Scandinavia, Chile, and others had been so crushingly negative that the draft itself had no future.

Fr. O'Hanlon commented that the writings on indulgences in the last thirty years had represented only the "new view," that the system of indulgences was understandable only from its history, that indulgences for the dead simply meant that the dead could be helped by prayer, and that with the present complications in the system, it might be best simply to let it go and build up the spiritual values for which it had been designed by other means. I should not be surprised if this represented the consensus of the more thoughtful leaders of the church.

Wednesday, November 17, 1965

There is little to report about the general congregation this morning, for the entire time was taken by the reading of the latter half of the last part of the *schema* on "The Church in the Modern World."

Dr. W. A. Visser t'Hooft of the World Council of Churches looked in this morning, as Dr. Edwin Espy had done yesterday. They are here for joint meetings of the international committee appointed by the Secretariat and the World Council of Churches.

As usual, after a section was read, a vote upon it was taken. Though there will be a good many amendments, they are not likely to affect the text to any great degree.

I note that the new text speaks variously about contemporary economic life. It lavishes no praise on the welfare state; includes white collar men with the others in its observations about workers; and condemns that type of anonymity in industries which makes it impossible to identify those responsible for policies.

On the matter of church and state, it declares that each is autonomous, but since they exist for the good of the same people they must devote their autonomy to cooperation.

In the matter of peace and war the text does away with distinctions between just and unjust wars, offensive and defensive wars, conventional and non-conventional arms, those who serve a warring nation with arms or in other ways, total war and "minor" wars—on the ground that the modern situation has altered these classical distinctions. It further asks the states to recognize the rights of conscientious objectors, provided they are willing to accept some other form of national service.

So the church moves ahead in its moral judgments.

At 4:15 this afternoon, the English-speaking observers met with their compatriots of the Secretariat to discuss the doctrine of the church regarding itself and, as usual, covered a good deal of ground and covered it fast. It was brought out by Fr. Norris that in the Constitution on the Church, adopted at the last session of the council, the kingdom of heaven and the church are no longer equated. Again, the true church is said to "subsist in the Roman Catholic Church"—which, again, is very different from saying that the true church *is* the Roman Catholic Church. Furthermore, the church is defined as *simul sancta et purificanda* (at once holy and in need of reform). This is so close to Martin Luther's *simul justus et peccator* (at once redeemed and still a sinner) that the comparison can be missed by no student of church history. Of course not all Roman Catholic interpreters would agree with Fr. Norris, but he is able to cite chapter and verse for his position.

After the English-speaking reunion, I met Mildred and we went together to the English mass, which is celebrated at Jesuit headquarters early every weekday evening in a form brought from Australia. Liturgically it was the high point of our whole experience here, for eight men concelebrated, including Frs. Dan O'Hanlon and Godfrey Diekmann. In most modern English ("The Lord be with you," "and with *you*," for instance, instead of the outworn and meaningless, "The Lord be with you," "and with *thy spirit*") and with other variations which drew people into the service it came astonishingly to life. Our heads being bowed, various members of the congregation suggested appropriate intercessions in single sentences ("That the nations may learn the ways of peace," for example) and the entire congregation combined its strength in a spoken and eager response, "O Lord, hear our prayer!" It was a strong marriage of individual longing and corporate communion. I was honored by being asked to read the Epistle—a Protestant at a Catholic mass. (But in all candor I must add that *since* the council, this practice has been disallowed by Rome.)

▱ *Thursday, November 18, 1965*

Today was held as important a public session as we have seen since the beginning of the council. It was important as a direction sign, showing the road the church is to take in the future under Pope Paul.

The music, under Bartolucci's leadership, was as usual supremely beautiful. In the alternate verses of the *Veni Creator Spiritus* the boy choir sang a fugal descant to the men's melody which carried us above the clouds. And at the end we all sang together the *Christus Vincit*.

It was the personnel of the concelebrants which gave us our first glimpse into tomorrow, for the Holy Father had selected for his aides, among the twenty-four, such men as Frs. Jean de Lubac, Sebastian Tromp, John Courtney Murray, and Johannes Feiner. Fr. de Lubac had been silenced some years ago largely through the influence, it is said, of Fr. Tromp, who was the trusted but very conservative theologian to Pope Pius XII. That they should have been asked to celebrate holy communion together declared, even louder than words could have done, that the church is now ready to listen to all its loyal thinkers, however they may differ on doctrines not yet fixed. John Courtney

Murray, not too long ago, had been told not to publish further on the subject of church and state, but he has now become the chief designer of the declaration on religious liberty, which the council takes up tomorrow. And Fr. Feiner of the Secretariat on Church Unity, and one of the interpreters for the observers, is the recent editor of an anthology of theological essays by some of the most forward-looking of Roman thinkers today. When he came in to lunch at the "Observatory" after the service, we gave him a round of proud applause. It takes no prophet or son of a prophet to understand what all this augurs for the church.

The Pope's allocution from the throne plotted the course of the future even more vividly.

He has already set up three commissions to implement the work of the council—one on the Sacred Liturgy, one for the revision of the code of Canon Law, and the third on Communications.

The episcopal synod will be called, if not next year, then certainly the year following. Nothing, as I have remarked before, could be more significant than this, for this marks a change in the very structure of the church's government.

The Roman curia will be appropriately reorganized through simplification and other types of improvement.

Within a short time a new statute will be published to provide new procedures for the principal sacred congregation, that of the Holy Office. At the announcement of this innovation a murmur ran through the great hall, as if 2,500 fathers had turned to their neighbors and said, "At last!"

The process of beatification of Popes Pius XII and John XXIII will be begun canonically forthwith. Here the applause was immediate and spontaneous. That from the seats of the observers was surely for John, who had conceived the council, but in the expansive mood of celebration the observers were not against casting honor in the way of Pius, as well, though some of them thought that the linking of the two was not without its political overtones. In fact, by afternoon the jest was going the rounds that the beatification of Pope Pius should be put down as one of the miracles of Pope John, clearly endorsing the latter for beatitude.

Applause followed two special announcements. One reported that in memory of the council the Pope will cause to be erected in one of the new areas of Rome (or at least a location dictated by pastoral needs) a church dedicated to Mary, "the Mother of the Church." And the other informed the delegates that a special jubilee for the entire church would begin at the closing of the council and last until next Pentecost. Jubilees have normally been seasons of unusual indulgences. Memories being still warm from the recent flare-up about indulgences, all will be awaiting with unalloyed curiosity the publication of the promised booklet that is to give information about the proposed jubilee.

There were two conciliar instruments promulgated today—the dogmatic Constitution on Divine Revelation and the Decree on the Apostolate of the Laity.

That on divine revelation is of special interest, for its history is virtually the history of the evolution of the mind of the council itself. The original *schema* on the subject was one of the first to reach the hands of the fathers at the very beginning of the council. It had been developed by a pre-conciliar commission uninfected by the biblical theology of today, nostalgic for those happy yesterdays when the *magisterium* of the church commanded an unreflecting obedience from all the faithful, and definitely fearful of the results that a scientific approach to the Bible record might have upon Rome. Examining some of the methods and attitudes accepted by leading biblical scholars throughout the Western world, it roundly condemned form criticism and its findings, and in general represented the scholarly thought of 1870 rather than that of 1962. Pope John appointed a joint commission to repair the document, and this commission, having worked effectively through the intervening years, was now able to witness the culmination and coronation of its work. Instead of putting out a declaration oriented to the past, which would have been an astonishment and hissing among scholars, the church today promulgated a constitution which casts light on the path into the future, and unites Roman scholarship with that of the best schools of the Western world.

📕 *Friday, November 19, 1965*

Word went round today that Fr. Yves Congar had also been invited to concelebrate with the Pope yesterday. Since he is another upon whom the Holy Office had once frowned, the invitation added still further significance to the occasion. He could not serve, unfortunately, because of his lameness.

The liturgy this morning was in the Hungarian rite, a Byzantine form. Remembering the Hungarian rhapsodies and the other emotion-packed music of the people of Hungary, I expected the music of this mass to be alive and vivid; but alas, it seemed quite uninspired, hardly matching the excitement of the mystery it accompanied.

Quite different was the music of the choir of St. Mary of the Valley from Subiaco. This was joyful, even sprightly. We were glad to have it interspersed between the votes on the document on religious liberty. No one can fail to note that though early in the week there was no time for any more possible fulminations against indulgences, on this last day there was time for listening to a neighborhood choir.

Speaking of lack of time, this morning Msgr. Arrighi (who has endeared himself to us all by his combination of efficiency and good humor) told us that with the final triumph of the *schema* on religious liberty, he had thought it appropriate that Bishop de Smedt should walk down the long nave of St. Peters with Miss Liberty on his arm, to be married at the high altar. He even volunteered to carry the lady's train. But he added that the Secretary General, to his great regret, had told him that there would be no time for this.

Bishop de Smedt did indeed introduce the final votes on the amendments to the famous declaration. This is the seventh time —the perfect number—that he has expressed himself on the subject in the council. Today he took up some of the criticisms of the fathers found in the amendments they had turned in.

Some of them apparently find the text in opposition to ecclesiastical documents put forth up to the time of Leo XII (and mimeographed and distributed by the "Carlists" here). Bishop de Smedt's point was that whereas pontifical documents up to that time emphasized the moral duties of public authority toward true religion, the recent thinkers of the church, while not compromising that emphasis, stressed the other duty of public authority, that of respecting the dignity of the human person in religious matters.

Some of the fathers wanted the reference to personal rights to be deleted from the text on the ground that religious liberty is no more than a positive civil right. But this would change the very substance of the document, and it would be dangerous to make the liberty of the church depend upon the will of state legislators.

Some feared that the appeal to "public order" might in an unfriendly state constitute a reason to restrict religious liberty, and in this connection preferred the term "common good." The bishop defended the use of the first phrase, however, on the ground that it is current in modern legislation, and he showed that the text went on to explain what it meant. He thought that so far as the document could do so, the now amended *schema* would serve, when finally promulgated, as a powerful instrument for freedom in religion.

The only part of his *relatio* in which he raised his voice was that in which he insisted that the changes the commission had admitted in no way jeopardized the document's fundamental principle.

The final votes on the *schema* on "The Church in the Modern World" were announced this morning. Even on chapter 5, which deals with war and peace and about which there had been so much talk, there were only 523 amendments.

The largest number of no votes on religious liberty were those taken on the entire *schema*—249. Even these were more than I expected. The diehards do not die. But it is now regarded as approved and will go to the Pope for promulgation on December 7. So this is a story with a happy ending.

Now for a ten-day recess.

THE NINTH WEEK

[NOVEMBER 30 - DECEMBER 4]

👁 *Tuesday, November 30, 1965*

Most of us had been looking forward to last week's recess as a time for relaxation and even for packing up, preparatory to departure; but as a matter of fact, no week has been more crowded with engagements. Since the end not only of the session, but of the council itself, draws near, the calendar involves not only our regular engagements but also all those that have been, but can no longer be, put off. So we have been thrashing about like a catch of fish in a net being pulled out of the water.

There have been social engagements—very delightful ones, too—with residents of Rome and other visitors. A week ago Saturday the Secretariat took all observers and their wives to the Odescalchi Castle on Lake Branciano, about twenty-five miles from Rome, where I wished I was a boy again to play with other boys on the parapets and spiral staircases within the walls of this fifteenth-century pile. At the various luncheons and dinners we have had opportunity to compare notes with others as to the meaning of the total council and the ending, good, bad, or indifferent, to which it is likely to come in the remaining few days of its existence. Whereas a week or so ago the council fathers seemed fatigued and even, to a degree, uninterested in consequences if only they could be released to go home, today, with the week of variety behind them and the promise of the actual

163

ending before them, there is a new resilience in evidence—and if they are feeling a flush of pride in the work they have accomplished, they are surely not without justification. There are still those who say that we must keep our fingers crossed until religious liberty has been made the law of the church, but the best guess is that this will go through without real difficulty, though the company of two hundred or so who want no religious liberty for erroneous belief will continue to vote no to the end, as a witness.

The theological talks that some of us have had with men like Fr. Godfrey Diekmann and Hans Küng have left us so optimistic about the resolution of old differences that we feel the need to guard against euphoria. During the last four years, we have seen the bishops move steadily in the direction of the thought of such men as these, and if the momentum in this direction continues, we are in for a period of restatement and reunderstanding among all Christians. These men know their Bible, but I am impressed even more by their knowledge of church history as a totality. They do not go back for their standards so much to individuals and to eras, as sectarians would do, but they see the expression of Christian thought as a living thing, in a process of developing its own inwardness. Until now I had never thought that I would look to Rome as the most flexible of all the churches that call themselves Catholic, but my fellow Protestant observers and I today are not far from taking that position. Rome has not the inferiority complex that some of the others have: it does not need, for instance, to cling to episcopal succession as the very essence of the faith, substituting symptom for substance. Rome feels that it has the essence of the faith— and can therefore allow the expressions of it to take care of themselves.

The reporters from the various periodicals of the world, some of them having been here from the beginning, some of them coming in for the last scene of the last act, are always interesting guests, bringing as well as receiving news.

For Thanksgiving Day Mildred and I went to dinner at the

American embassy. There Ambassador and Mrs. Frederick Reinhardt had gathered together thirty or forty of the embassy family and other families in Rome, especially those with children.
We were delighted to see the latter, and by them were made to
realize how long and uninterruptedly we had been living in the
stilted world of adulthood. We thought the spirit of the Reinhardt family not the least gift of American diplomacy to Italy.

Stuart Anderson of the Pacific School of Religion having arrived in the course of the week to serve as the last of the observers from the International Congregational Council, I took
him this morning to the general congregation, where the mass
was celebrated according to the Maronite rite. The Pope was
present. He came in after all the rest of us were seated, but
most unobtrusively, walking the length of the nave like any
other bishop, and freely bestowing his blessing on the way.
Everybody is guessing what new announcement he will make on
the final day. Surely some sort of honor should come to the
secretaries and others who have worked hard for the success
of the council. Perhaps the former will be made cardinals.

Announcement was made that this Saturday a special service
for church unity would be held in the basilica of St. Pauls-outside-the-Walls, where Pope John XXIII originally announced the
calling of Vatican II. In this service even the observers are to
participate. Who, four years ago, would have dreamed that we
could have gone this far! The effect of this service will be felt
in interchurch relations throughout the world.

The morning was devoted to the final edition of "The Missionary Activity of the Church." The amendments accepted were
announced by the Very Rev. John Schütte, chairman of the commission dealing with the document. He spoke also of the proposed amendments that had not been accepted, in two of which
I was especially interested. Many of the fathers had wanted to
see the text written so that it would assure the presence, in the
Congregation for the Propagation of the Faith, of bishops and
others who have personal knowledge of missions, but the commission seems inclined to leave these matters of personnel as

much as possible in the hands of the Holy Father. Less liberal elements had wanted to rewrite and weaken the ecumenical suggestions in the text, but the members of the commission, I am glad to say, stood their ground at this point. The decree on missionary activity will therefore be an instrument of increasing usefulness in the hands of men of cooperative mind on the mission field.

Votes were taken on the document chapter by chapter. I am sure that no impressive minorities will be developed at this point.

Among the announcements made by the Secretary General this morning, one was to the effect that the computing machine used to total the vote in the public session of November 18 had mutilated thirty-six of the ballots. These, fortunately, were on the relatively uncontroverted matter of the apostolate of the laity. If the machines had shown their latent antipathy and spirit of vandalism on such a matter as religious liberty, the announcement might have been greeted by something besides the laughter which actually occurred. Fortunately, all the torn ballots were identifiable as affirmative.

This afternoon, as on Tuesday afternoon a week ago, the observers had their regular meeting with the Secretariat. At the former was discussed the Pope's latest encyclical, *Mysterium fidei,* which deals with the Eucharist. At the time this came out, as I have remarked, it seemed something like a rebuff to progressive thinkers, but it is now being generally interpreted as a kind of warning not to these thinkers but to those who draw wrong inferences from what these thinkers have written. The theme for this afternoon was mixed marriages. Actually, little is to be said about this at the moment, since the matter is in the hands of the Pope, to be set forth in the canon law in due time. I did not attend this meeting, since Mildred and I had been asked to represent the International Congregational Council at a reception given by the president of the republic. And thereafter we went to the reception at the American embassy given by Ambassador and Mrs. Reinhardt to all the Americans associated with the council.

📖 *Thursday, December 2, 1965*

Yesterday was a recess from everything but activity. In the morning Ghana visas had to be applied for on the other side of town; and the afternoon and evening were full too.

In the afternoon a meeting was held at the Waldensian College which may prove to have more meaning for the future than any other meetings that have been held here, save those associated with the council itself. The question before the twelve or fourteen representatives of various non-Roman denominations throughout the world gathered there was whether the time had now come for the establishment in Rome of a study institute on Roman Catholicism. It was unanimously agreed that it had. The United Church of Christ, for instance, is proposing to send to Rome some of its more promising young men to learn not only Roman doctrine but Roman procedures—Roman "life," in a word. There has been some question as to whether the Waldensian Church was as yet equipped to furnish leadership for such an enterprise, for not a little of the literature that has come from their presses during the last years has maintained the old, negative, anti-Roman tone. The faculty of the college under its dean, Prof. Valdo Vinay, however, seems to have breathed the new atmosphere and to have moved on into new and happy relationships with the faculties of the Roman Catholic institutions hereabout. It seems natural and right, therefore, that the non-Roman groups interested in sending men to Rome for the study of the Holy See, should turn to this faculty for leadership in establishing an institute, not under its wing, but in close association with it. Though this will be slow in development, the first step was taken yesterday.

Last night we went to the opera with Bill Norgren to enjoy Verdi's *Don Carlo*. It will be remembered that this is the opera that portrays the Spanish Inquisition in colors of stark and vivid terror. The theological ground on which this horrid organization was based was that error has no rights—precisely the same argument that sustains the hard core of opposition to the council's declaration on religious liberty. Though the Inquisition has grown less cruel during the centuries, the theory that has nourished it has only today, in the pronouncement of Vatican II, been brought to the end of its authority.

This morning Archbishop Marty of Reims introduced to the assembled fathers the amendments of the *schema* on "The Ministry and Life of Priests." No changes of real consequence were proposed. The document adheres closely to the Constitution on the Church. Many fathers had requested that it omit reference to the married priests of the Eastern churches, perhaps on the ground that any reference to the fact of a non-celibate priesthood would set loose dangerous thoughts in the minds of the Western hierarchy—but the commission fortunately held that a universal decree must be valid for the universal church, and left the references in the text. In the voting, the document was overwhelmingly approved.

Because time is getting short, the *relatio* on "The Church in the Modern World" was also read this morning—by Archbishop Garrone of Toulouse. He said his commission had correctly anticipated that most of the amendments would be on three matters —atheism, marriage, and war. And the commission had treated these three human calamities [not his word] with equal care.

Over five hundred fathers had wanted the commission to link atheism to communism, and condemn them both roundly. Be it said to the honor of the commission members that they had refused to do this. Nothing shows more clearly the difference between this council and many that have preceded it, than this: without retreating from its position that it possesses the truth, or at least is possessed by the truth, the church is unwilling to regard even its avowed enemies as completely devoid of truth; condemnation is giving way to a new reasonableness.

Some of the fathers had wanted the commission to sketch a blueprint for birth control, but this also the commission had refused to do. It is hoped that the Pope's commission on the subject will give this adequate treatment, but progressive voices hereabouts are saying that the commission has been given very little money to spend on getting itself together and that for a long time it has done nothing at all. One hopes that when the council is over it will be summoned to get on with its work.

The paragraph about conscientious objection in the war section of the document has apparently suffered from the Italian political situation—an indication that the Roman church has still some distance to go before it becomes truly universal. It is said that there are over fifty conscientious objectors in the Italian jails at the present time—and the text, alas, now reads not that men have a *right* to conscientious objection, but that in their conscientious objection they should be treated kindly!

The text on total war has been revised to meet the objection of those who have wanted more said about the right of self-defense. In the discussion of the armaments race, all references have been omitted that might seem offensive to particular nations—though why the church should go to school to the nations is difficult to see. All in all, I am afraid that we must say that the text, though still strong and rugged in spots, has been weakened.

This afternoon and evening we went to a series of gatherings with small groups. At the home of Mr. and Mrs. Israel Shenker of *Time* magazine, we had good conversation with them and their guests, Mr. Elson of the magazine's department of religious news, Bishop Blomjous of Africa, and Frs. Häring and Mejia, I think that I can truly say, though I am an extreme Protestant, that there is not a theological thought in my head which I have not found to be shared by some member of the Roman Catholic hierarchy.

Yesterday was another day when we had nothing to do officially and everything to do unofficially.

After a morning of letter writing and shopping, I went to a
lecture at the Gregorian University by Msgr. Davis on a man
who has been a subject of his study for his whole life—John
Henry Cardinal Newman. It takes a man of Davis' breadth to
understand a man of breadth like Newman, and I was especially
glad to hear this contemporary interpretation by the quiet and
discerning scholar next to whom I have sat at the council for
four years.

In the evening we had Cardinal Suenens for dinner at the Observatory. Since he is soon to visit America, we gathered about
him at one table the observers from Canada and the United
States. He was full of reminiscences of events of the council
which now become history, and having seen them from the point
of view of a cardinal and moderator, he showed them to us in a
new luminescence.

There was the motion of Cardinal Liénart at the very beginning, for instance, which (as all agree today) was nothing short
of an act of salvation for the council. Had he not asked for sufficient time to be given the fathers to consider and make their
selections of possible members on the various commissions of the
council, a slate would have been quickly adopted composed almost wholly of the Old Guard, to the neglect of the newer and
dynamic minds which have actually given the council its great-
ness. And I had not known before that Cardinal Liénart had
asked Cardinal Tisserant, then presiding, to recognize him for
this motion, that his request had been denied, and that in consequence Cardinal Liénart, as one of the presidents, had simply
taken the floor on his own and laid the all-important matter before the fathers. One trembles to think what would have come of
the council if this slight man from Lille had not been a combination of common sense and courage.

Cardinal Suenens was one of the living links between Pope John and Pope Paul, providing continuity to the council and keeping it a unity. I well remember a speech he made toward the end of the first session in which he outlined a plan for the corporate work of the council, calling for a systematic consideration, first, of the church in itself, then of its relationship with other Christians and other religions, and finally of its outreach into the secular world. (Allusion to this speech will be found on page 182 of my diary for 1962.) I well remember, also, that Cardinal Montini had approved the plan in a speech of his own the next day. But what I had not known was that the two cardinals had worked on the plan together, had submitted it to Pope John, had woven into it the comments of the latter (scribbled in his own hand in Italian on the margins of the draft), and had therefore been able to make it public in the full assurance of speaking virtually *ex cathedra*. When now it is recalled that Cardinal Montini presently became Pope Paul VI, and in his opening allocution at the second session outlined virtually the same plan for the work of the council, it will be seen that the church owes not a little to the intelligent initiative of Cardinal Suenens.

Readers of my diary of the second session will remember that we on the outside were surprised that there should be so long an interval between the time when the famous Five Questions were proposed and when they were actually voted upon. These questions—which were an adroit way of securing the mind of the majority of the council to serve as a lever of influence within commissions where militant minorities were dominant—were introduced by Cardinal Suenens. He introduced them on his own, without consulting the Secretary General, Archbishop Felici, for he knew that if he had done so, they would never have seen the light. (We on the outside who see the archbishop only as a master of ceremonies and of situations, have not known him, as many of the council fathers have, as a master also of parliamentary controls. Archbishop Roberts the other day, for instance, though he had well over the necessary seventy backers for a speech after the debate had closed, was not given the privilege of utterance.) When therefore the proposal of the Five Questions was made, it immediately struck opposition in the procedural committee. For a long time it was nip and tuck as to whether the questions would be reported out or not. The progressives finally won the one-man majority necessary by counting as a sign of affirmation the uplifted hand of a gesticulating Italian member who at the moment did not realize that the committee was voting—or so the story goes.

Today the votes on the *schema* on the priesthood were published—with a negligible number of negatives.

The order of the day was the voting on *schema* 13. Here the prophecy was that everything would go smoothly—until, in the course of the morning, we became aware that the whispered conversations throughout the council were on the subject of a printed letter signed by Cardinal Spellman and others and circulated to all the fathers asking that they vote no on chapter 5 because of its condemnation of total war. This was a shock to the progressives, who feared that an expanded negative vote on this chapter would cause the commission to blot out sundry paragraphs and reduce the whole document to the limpness of a rag. Having seen eleventh-hour attempts of this sort fail in the past, I told myself that there was nothing to fear, though in reality I feared the worst. However, as we learned late this afternoon, the conservative brethren, though marshaled by as doughty an organizer as Bishop Hannan, had failed to chalk up a total of more than 483 negative votes.

In an interval between votes this morning, the message from the observers to the council (for which I had agitated against some opposition on our executive committee, which none of the rest of us understood) was read aloud by the Secretary General and received with the greatest enthusiasm. It was a word of gratitude written originally in German by Dr. Lukas Vischer, reviewed by some others of us, and translated into Latin for the benefit of all.*

---

* See Appendix I at the end of this diary.

This afternoon came one of the crowning events of the council—a "sacred celebration for the promotion of unity among Christians." This was held, symbolically, at St. Pauls-outside-the-Walls where Pope John, early in 1959, had made the original announcement that there would be a Vatican Council. All of us observers were invited by the Benedictines of the monastery associated with the basilica to come to lunch and spend the afternoon in their spacious halls. This we did, not missing the small room where Pope John told the cardinals then in Rome, who had gathered with him there to help him celebrate the Feast of the Conversion of St. Paul, what he was about to proclaim publicly in the great basilica—that a council of all the bishops of the world would be held to legislate the *aggiornamento* of the forms and procedures of the church.

Now in that same basilica, at five o'clock, the Holy Father, the cardinals, the patriarchs, and the council fathers gathered *with the observers* to dedicate themselves in common to the uniting of all who call themselves Christian. The Pope did not preside, but he did deliver a brief homily, expressing his own concern for the unity of Christendom. He concluded by comparing contemporary Christianity to the scholar who, locked in a monastery, had to walk up and down all night in the dark waiting for the dawn, which would show him what door to open. With the Pope we all hoped that the dawn would show us the new door to unity—and this was brought out in the parts of the worship itself. This time there was no master of rites flitting about, telling the participants where to stand and when to speak, for the whole service was simplicity itself, consisting of a hymn (we all sang "Now Thank We All Our God" in English), psalms, readings by Catholics and non-Catholics (Dr. Outler and Fr. Maan representing the observers), and prayers, mostly prayers. I suppose that this was the first time in his life that the Holy Father had participated in a formal service of the sort with Protestants. These are the first rays of the new morning to which the Pope pointed, and the light from this service at Rome will illuminate and make the ecumenical way easier in every diocese of the world.

After the service we followed the Pope into an adjacent room where, after greetings presented by Cardinal Bea and (on behalf of us observers) the Lord Bishop of Ripon, he himself responded briefly in several languages and then placed in the hands of each one of us in turn a beautifully printed "diploma" commemorating our presence here, and a hand-wrought bronze table bell.

THE LAST DAYS

[DECEMBER 6-8]

✎ *Monday, December 6, 1965*

Last night I went for dinner to the apartment of the Paulist Fathers near the Church of Santa Susanna, of which they are in charge. Every Sunday evening while the council has been in session they have invited observers and other friends in for a rich evening of conversation. This is one of their many ministries for which we feel no end of gratitude.

The 168th and last general congregation of the Second Ecumenical Vatican Council was held this morning. On my cuff I was able to figure that if we have had an average of fifteen speakers per congregation, I have listened to 2,500 bursts of oratory—and fifteen is a low average.

The mass was in the Byzantine-Ruthenian rite of North America, which is to say that it was *sung* in *American English*. The melodies of the chants were, to be sure, brought over from the Old World, serving as a connecting link between the centuries past and *aggiornamento*. But the language had the unmistakable accent of Pittsburgh, the celebrant being our friend Bishop Elko of the Ruthenian rite of that city. This was just one more proof to me that the vernacular is here to stay, for this service was understandable, even to strangers.

The service, by the way, has its own interesting history, for

175

its use—with its non-ecclesiastical language—was originally forbidden by the Holy Office; but this ban was in turn overruled by Pope John XXIII, in anticipation of the action by the council.

Even we observers felt drawn into the service, for special prayers were lifted up for us.

I am afraid that the agitation, chiefly American, to vote down the chapter in which the church refuses to give its blessing to total war, has not advanced the standing of the American hierarchy in the eyes of the world. This morning when Cardinal Shehan, Archbishop Krol, and Bishop Hannan were huddled about Secretary of State Cicognani, a European priest near me pointed to them and smilingly said, "The peace lovers"—an unfair slur, but a reflection of a general sentiment derived from reading the letter circulated two days ago by Cardinal Spellman and others.

This morning, in the hands of many, there was a letter sent out by the commission that had worked on this chapter. It was designed to refute the arguments of the letter of last Saturday —and that it succeeded is proved by the fact that the vote on the whole *schema,* including the chapter on war, taken this morning, showed only 251 negatives—and toward the end of the morning it was announced that the Holy Father had telephoned that he was ready to promulgate the now famous *schema* 13 tomorrow as a Pastoral Constitution.

The order of the morning dragged on slowly, for it was necessary not only to distribute a good deal of literature but also to give to each one of the fathers a diploma and a gold ring, from the Pope. The bull declaring and regulating the extraordinary jubilee which is to follow the council was read in full by the Secretary General.

At the end, thanks were expressed to all who had in any way contributed to the success of the council. Archbishop Felici read his thanks to the fathers in Latin verse, to the delight of all. Cardinal Suenens, presiding, returned the thanks of the council to the *"Secretarius Generalis Extraordinarius,"* and in the course of further expressions of gratitude asked the pardon of

the fathers for having called so many of them to time for speaking too long: "We expect ample absolution for this free confession!"

The observers also shared in this overflow of friendly spirit,
mention of them being greeted with prolonged applause.

Two events have recently taken place outside the council which
could hardly have happened had it not been for the council.

Yesterday announcement was made simultaneously in Istanbul
and Rome that following conversations which were initiated by
the Pope and the Ecumenical Patriarch in Jerusalem in January
of last year, an agreement has been arrived at which will "remove
both from memory and from the midst of the church the sentences of excommunication" which were leveled by the Eastern
and Western churches against each other in the eleventh century. December 7—tomorrow, when the Vatican Council will hold
its final public session—has been chosen as the day when this
new mutual declaration of understanding will be formally announced. For the relations between Rome and Eastern Orthodoxy this is a step of infinite significance.

And today it was announced by the Pope in a *motu proprio*
—an official personal statement—how the Holy Office would be
reorganized. From now on it will be known as "The Congregation for the Doctrine of the Faith" or, as we might say, "The
Commission on Christian Doctrine." There is no longer to be
any "commissar" perpetuating the figure of the Grand Inquisitor.
To meet given situations, it will call together groups of experts,
and it will no longer condemn doctrines as contrary to the faith
without advance advice from the bishops concerned. In passing
judgments upon errors deemed contrary to the faith, it will follow the norms of ordinary legal procedure. This puts an end to
condemning a man without a hearing. And to all these innova-
tions it will add that of keeping in touch with the papal commission on biblical studies and in general involving the profes-
sors of the university in its inquiries. So another era comes to an
end and a better day begins to brighten the eastern horizon.

This afternoon, at a reception given by the observers to the

Secretariat, the various church families which we represent each presented a book considered to be representative of it for the beginning of a Secretariat library. Ralph Calder of the International Congregational Council had ordered from the United States Williston Walker's *Creeds and Platforms of Congregationalism*—which arrived on Friday, just in time for me to have it bound in Italian parchment with a suitable inscription in gold on the cover.

This evening at eight we who have been living at the Hotel Castel Sant'Angelo—who constitute a large majority of the observers—all dined together to do honor to the five Roman Catholic interpreters who live with us, Frs. Carbon (French), Feiner (German), Novack (Greek), Norris and O'Hanlon (both Americans). Speeches were made, small gifts given, and a good time had by all. The rarified intellectual atmosphere of the affair may be gauged from the limericks presented regarding the two Americans:

> To Frank the handsome son of Norris
> Who never ceases working for us
>   All of us here
>   Now loud and clear
> Join in a Hallelujah Chorris.
>
> There was an O'Hanlon named Dan
> A vitally versatile man
>   No task was too large
>   For him to discharge:
> He's the popular pride of our clan.

The verses about the others were, if anything, even more atrocious as poetry than these, though equally cordial in intent.

We have come to hold these men in warmest affection, for they have served us at every turn. They have been centers around which our fine camaraderie at the Observatory has been built up. We are glad the council is over, but sorry to contemplate the breakup of this happy fraternity.

ᗡ *Tuesday, December 7, 1965*

The great final public session this morning followed the lines of that held on November 18. Four promulgations were made—of the Declaration on Religious Liberty, of the Decree on the Missionary Activity of the Church and the Decree on the Ministry and Life of Priests, and of the Pastoral Constitution on the Church in the Modern World. The Pope's allocution was a homily in the true sense of the word, a quiet expression of gratitude, encouragement, and challenge to his people.

The extraordinary event, anticipated since yesterday, was the appearance of the Metropolitan of Constantinople, representing the Ecumenical Patriarch, who received from the Holy Father a magnificently illuminated parchment signalizing the reconciliation and rapprochement of the two churches. One concomitant of this episode was especially heartwarming, for it had in it a dash of spontaneity. When the Holy Father and Metropolitan Meliton embraced each other, the presiding deacon called for the kiss of peace from all—and the bishops throughout the great hall embraced and shook hands with their neighbors on each side. It was a moving act of solidarity.

One could not but compare the smooth, serene, and spiritual closing of this council with that of Vatican I. In 1870, on the final day, a thunderstorm swept over the city and darkened St. Peters to such a degree that candles had to be brought to read by. Today, on the other hand, a shaft of warm sunlight from the high window in the south transept flooded the altar with light while the Pope and twenty-four presidents of episcopal conferences throughout the world were concelebrating the Holy Eucharist.

It was not all sunshine, however. The intransigeants held out to the end: there were 70 noes on "Religious Liberty" and 75 on "The Church in the Modern World."

We learned later that Archbishop Iakovos of New York was

present for the ceremony of rapprochement—as was also Archbishop Nikodim, the head of the church in Russia. Indeed, we
had the latter as a guest at the Observatory last night. And today at luncheon, which was a banquet of eleven overflowing
courses, a farewell given us by the proprietor and manager of
our *pensione,* there was present my old friend Dr. Hromadka of
Czechoslovakia.

This afternoon we attended our last session with the Secretariat.
Bishop Willebrands took the chair and talked to us informally
about his impressions of the council and his hopes for the future. He referred to the philosophy that had guided the council in its early days—that, though truth does not change, the expressions of truth must be changed to meet the needs of suc-
cessive ages. Hence *aggiornamento.* Looking back on the council from the vantage point of these last days, however, (said the
bishop) we perceive that much more has changed than the expression of truth: our perception of truth is deeper, fuller. He
expressed the kind judgment that the presence of observers,
who had come more and more to occupy the position of consultants, had had something to do with the deepening of the insights of the council. He spoke of the feeble beginnings in common prayer which we had had but which, under the touch of
the Holy Spirit, had now reached an apogee in the service of
last Saturday. "Church history has now become our *common*
history: the day of private Roman Catholic history, or private
non-Roman Catholic history of the church, is now done." Bishop
Silen asked, half jokingly, half seriously, about the apostolic constitution proclaiming the special jubilee at the end of the council. He pointed out that special indulgences were to be given
to those who truly repented of having sinned by reading books
of "heretics and schismatics"—books, that is, written by Protestants (like this diary). Bishop Willebrands said simply that he
did not know the inwardness of the purpose which included in a
document of today these phrases of yesterday, but he feared
that the paragraph emanated from an office not in touch with
real life.

On behalf of us all Dr. Vischer presented an old medal of 1730 to Bishop Willebrands, a medal struck to commemorate the Protestant Reformation. Said he, "We cannot very well cast away such a medal as this, with its memories, but we can recast it— and that we now propose to do."

✍ *Wednesday, December 8, 1965*

The heavens smiled on the last day of the council. Scudding clouds only now and then shut off the sunshine which warmed the one hundred thousand people gathered in the piazza before St. Peters and made vivid the white of the vestments of Pope, cardinals, and bishops.

The service was for the most part in Latin, though some of the liturgy (perhaps as a nod of greeting to the Eastern churches) was in Greek. A high mass was followed by the solemn ceremony of closing the council: here the declarations intended for the world were in French.

At the high moment of the mass, as on a previous occasion, brasses broke into a paean. To mark the death of Christ by this means still seems to me a phenomenal piece of insensitivity, but it must be said that today this was greatly mitigated, since the morning breezes and the holiday spirit of the crowd left little of worship in the ears and minds of any—except possibly the Pope, who celebrated.

As part of the service the Pope placed checks amounting to $90,000 in the hands of five bishops representing Palestine, Argentina, Southern India, Pakistan, and Cambodia—countries where the need for charity today is very great.

A feature interesting to me was the special word of recognition and encouragement given by one of the cardinals on behalf of the Pope to each of several groups in the human family. For

each category there were a few persons on hand to represent
their fellows through the world—government leaders, intellectuals
(Jacques Maritain being one of the recipients actually present),
artists, women, workers (one of those who approached the Pope's
throne being dressed in the coveralls of a mechanic), youth
(though according to the European theory of youth, not one of
the recipients appeared to be less than forty years of age), and
the sick and the poor (one of these being paraplegic and another a blind man, whose Seeing Eye dog, accompanying him,
also received a blessing from the Holy Father).

In the closing rite the Pope blessed the first stone of the new
parish church that is to be constructed in one of the growing
suburbs of Rome in memory of the Second Vatican Council.

In the booklet placed in our hands describing, in French, the
order of service, it referred to the traditional manner of closing
all councils from Chalcedon to Trent—with acclamations. This
was no exception but, actually, how different were these acclamations from any that had ever gone before! Trent, for instance,
had been a veritable Mount Ebal, whence went forth cursings.
It ended with a cardinal crying,

Anathema to all heretics!

and the fathers responding,

Anathema! Anathema!

The only *damnandum est* I can recall in any of the promulgations of Vatican II is the one condemning total war.

Vatican II has been a Gerizim, a Mount of Blessings. Its last
moments were given to scattering over the world not fire and
brimstone but prayers for peace and expressions of goodwill.
Among the many intercessions we who had represented the non-
Roman churches were moved to hear the great council chant, in
Latin:

Upon the Christian churches and communities which in brotherhood have sent observers to our assembly, let rest peace and
love in the unity of the Spirit!

Not exactly like Trent!

In fact nothing could have brought out more clearly the fundamental *aggiornamento* of the council. Secondary forms along a wide front have been altered to make them understandable to the modern world, but here was something far from secondary: for what could be more basic than the church's own conception of itself, its own consciousness of what it is and what it was put into the world to accomplish? The Roman Catholic Church is now to be seen not as the forbidding and unbending continuity of the Roman Empire, defended inside and out with legalities, as many have conceived it to be: no, it is a company of faithful people gathered around the altar of Christ ready to carry the things of Christ to the world in ministry.

With the words of the Pope,

In the name of the Lord Jesus Christ, go in peace!

and the response of the mighty company,

Thanks be to God!

the work of the council came to an end. Came to an end? It is just the beginning.

Appendix I

*Message of the Observers to the Council Fathers,
to Whom It Was Given in Latin
December 4, 1965*

REVEREND COUNCIL FATHERS:

Now that the end of Vatican Council II is approaching, the observers and guests of the Secretariat for Christian Unity are moved to express to you the gratitude they feel in looking back on the notable and important events which they have witnessed.

We accepted the invitation to the council in order that we might observe its labors more intimately and carry the news of it to our churches. Everywhere we have been most cordially received. Innumerable marks of friendship, love, and esteem have been shown us. The good word *dialogue,* which we have heard so often, is no longer empty but has been filled with content. Again and again opportunities for personal meetings and conversations have been offered. Although the council fathers as well as the *periti* have been burdened with work, they have been truly solicitous to acquire a deeper understanding of the beliefs of other churches. The personal ties which have bound us to you in these years will be treasured by us forever.

This is not the moment to discuss in detail the council and the results it has achieved in these years. But we should like to take the occasion to make it clear to the council fathers that we have not viewed the work of the council, as it were, at a distance but have followed it closely in all intellectual eagerness; for what happens in one church is of concern to all the others as well. In the course of the sessions this insight has become clearer and clearer. In spite of their division the churches remain nonetheless united in the name of Christ. We observers are firmly persuaded that the communion achieved so far can and will grow deeper. In the first audience given to the observers, Pope John of happy memory quoted the words of the Psalmist: Blessed be the Lord who daily loadeth us with benefits (Ps. 68:19)! These words may now be repeated in the form: Blessed be the Lord for all the benefits which through his Spirit he has given us to this day, and for all those which he purposes to give us in the future!

Appendix II

This was written at the suggestion made by Pastor Marc Boegner on September 21, 1965, and sent to Bishop Wille-brands in the thought that the Pope and the Roman Catholic leadership in general would be glad to have a non-Roman Christian judgment on a subject upon which decision was soon to be made. The original was in French.

Various observers and guests of the council, responding to the kind suggestion of His Holiness, Pope Paul VI, desire to submit a few considerations on the subject of mixed marriages. They limit themselves to the area of marriage between baptized Christians, regarding whom the Decree on Ecumenism says: "All who have been justified by faith in baptism are incorporated into Christ; they therefore have a right to be called Christians, and with good reason are accepted as brothers by the children of the Catholic Church" (*Decretum de Oecumenismo*, #3).

The undersigned see mixed marriage as a difficult pastoral problem which takes shape especially in relation to the Roman Catholic Church. They recognize that this problem cannot be wholly resolved as long as the churches are separated. At the same time they feel that it is the task of all churches to strive to solve or at least to lessen the problem. They therefore regard the proposals of Section 5 of the *votum* regarding the sacrament of marriage, discussed by the council on the 19th and 20th of November, 1964, as an advance step in the present situation.

The observers and guests whose names appear below give special emphasis to the following four proposals of the *votum:*

1) The question of mixed marriages should be taken up in the spirit of the Decree on Ecumenism and the Declaration on Religious Liberty.

2) The directions regarding the marriage of a Roman Catholic with a baptized non-Roman Catholic and those regarding marriage with an unbaptized person should be separated.

3) The present law excommunicating those Catholics who contract marriage before a non-Catholic minister should be repealed.

4) The bishop ordinary should be given the right in particular cases to waive the requirement of the canonical form for marriage if by that means validity may be maintained for the marriage of persons genuinely willing to be married which is publicly celebrated in another form.

With grateful recognition of these reliefs proposed in the *votum* it seems to the undersigned that the spirit of the Decree on Ecumenism and of the Declaration on Religious Liberty calls for freedom for responsibly Christian parents to decide as to the confession in which their children are to be baptized and reared.

The undersigned are convinced that the burning problem of mixed marriage cannot be resolved once for all between the churches but that it must be clarified in the light of further ecumenical developments. The questions as to the end and nature of marriage which are today being considered so earnestly in the Roman Catholic Church are similarly a concern to the other churches. They are striving to maintain in theory and practice the indissolubility of marriage as Christ desired it. If the imminent papal *motu proprio* appears in a form which provides for future ecumenical dialogue on this subject, the churches will undoubtedly be in a position, in the rising atmosphere of mutual trust, to work out further resolutions of this question together. Signed by:

APPENDIX

Marc Boegner
Honorary President of the Protestant Federation of Churches in France

Kristen Ejnar Skydsgaard
Professor of Systematic Theology, University of Copenhagen, Denmark

Edmund Schlink
Professor of Dogmatics, University of Heidelberg, Germany

Heiko A. Oberman
Professor of Church History, Harvard University Divinity School, U. S. A.

Oscar Cullmann
Professor at the Universities of Basel, Switzerland, and Paris, France

Lukas Vischer
Research Secretary, Commission on Faith and Order, World Council of Churches

Warren A. Quanbeck
Professor of Systematic Theology, Luther Theological Seminary, St. Paul, U. S. A.

L. J. van Holk
Professor at the University of Leiden, The Netherlands

P. J. Maan
Vicar of the Cathedral Church of Utrecht, The Netherlands

Douglas Horton
Former Moderator of the International Congregational Council

José Miguez-Bonino
Director of the Evangelical Theological Faculty of Buenos Aires, Argentina

Hébert Roux
In charge of Interconfessional Relations, Protestant Federation of France

Vilmos Vajta
Director of Lutheran Ecumenical Institute, Strasbourg, France

Roger Schutz
Prior, Community of Taizé, France

†Metropolite Emilianos
Metropolitan of Calabria

Professeur Paul Evdomikov
Orthodox Theological Institute, St. Serge, Paris, France

†Archimandrite Maximos Aghiorgoussis
Rector of the Greek Orthodox Parish, Rome, Italy

†Evêque Karekin Sarkissian
Dean of the Armenian Theological Seminary, Anteias, Lebanon

†John Moorman
Bishop of Ripon, England

Harold Roberts
Principal of Richmond Theological College, England

John Findlow
The Archbishop of Canterbury's Representative, Rome, Italy

Wolfgang Dietzfelbinger
Pastor of Erbendorf, Germany

Appendix III

This is the statement I made on behalf of the observers on the occasion of Cardinal Bea's reception to us on September 18, 1965. Since it expresses the feelings we have for the entire Secretariat for Christian Unity, to which these diaries were originally dedicated, it seems appropriate to let it appear here as the diaries' last word.

Allow me, Your Eminence, to say a word which, though it comes from my lips, speaks the sentiment of all of us observers. You have opened to us many doors.

To speak of the most immediate matter, you have opened to us the door which has admitted us to this charming reception. . . . Your receptions . . . bring together, in most attractive surroundings, people of a common interest, who enjoy each other and carry away from each other's conversations memories which linger with them long and pleasantly. For this we thank you.

But you have also opened to us the door of St. Peters. I think that most of us, in reporting the council, try to drop the information with light nonchalance, almost as if we did not know we were saying it, that we observers are allowed to enter the basilica by the entrance used by the cardinals. And when on the first day we found our way to the place of our assignment, we discovered that our seats were not good ones at all: they were simply the best seats in the hall, thanks to your door-open-

191

ing magic. It is hardly surprising that one bishop, whose seat
is at the eastern end of the basilica, is said to have remarked,
"I am going to leave the church and come back as an observer
in order to be able to see what is going on."

But our place under the protective spear of St. Longinus is
only a single illustration of your continuing and unstinted concern for us. To us comes the same literature that goes to the
council fathers themselves; to us it is given to hear every debate
in the aula, to which we listen eloquently—but if we miss the
meaning of the Latin, to us it is also given to turn to translators
close by and hear the truth repeated to us in the language of
Trafalgar Square, the Champs Elysées, the Red Square, or any
of several other contemporary outposts of the Tower of Babel.
And these translators, by the way, have become more to us than
simple retailers of speech: they have proved to be interpreters
of men and relationships, uncovering to us the inner richness,
including the creative tensions, of the council, which we could
only have conjectured without them. Some of us have the advantage of living at the Hotel de luxe Castel Sant'Angelo, which
overshadows the Hilton for good comradeship and opportunity
for illuminating discussion. We are indeed coming to know each
other so well that you may be said to be responsible for a new
burst of ecumenism among non-Roman Christians. And crowning all there is the chance for talking things over with the Secretariat at our weekly meetings. These are the spice that is added
to the banquet of St. Peters. Through these conferences we feel
drawn into the heart of the council itself. Often our ideas re-
appear a few days later on the floor of St. Peters, carried there
through your arrangement by some good courier of like mind.
Always we are met in the conferences with open-minded candor,
and we have been indeed most grateful to enter through this
door.

Most of all, we are indebted to you for opening the door of
your friendship. Now there are a few differences of theology
and polity which have developed between the Roman church
and the rest of us during the centuries in which we have been

studying how to keep separate. We shall have to trust the generations, not to say centuries, to come, to give us opportunity to
resolve them; but it is evident to all that thanks to the friendship you have shown us, the ground is now laid out of which
reconciliations can grow. As a theologian you may call friendship
a non-theological factor, but, theological or not, friendship must
have a part to play in the future of the church. The historian
can easily show that unhappy non-theological factors went into
the great divisions of the church—economic and political rivalries
and the like—and if that is the case, then the happy non-theological factor of friendship can play its part in the reintegration of
Christendom. Because you have made us your friends, nothing
important to you can be unimportant to us: we shall never again
be indifferent (however we may disagree) to anything in your
theology, your polity, your liturgy. Let this relationship of simple
human friendship be carried from the center you have created
here to the boundaries of Christendom and we shall have at
least the beginnings of ecumenism.

I said at the beginning that though mine was the voice speaking, the words came from all of us observers. In closing, let me
add that though my words are directed to your ears, we should
not be sorry to have them reach the hearts of all your loyal aides
in the Secretariat, for they are intended for them as well. But
please keep some of our gratitude for yourself: so far as we observers are concerned, *Beatitudo* begins with *Bea*.

INDEX

198

VATICAN DIARY 1965

Findlow, John, Canon, Anglican Communion 79, 143

Flores Martin, Jaimé, Bishop 118

Florit, Ermenegildo Cardinal 113, 129

Frings, Joseph Cardinal 19, 51, 73

Frotz, Agostino, Bishop 74

Garcia Lahiguera, José, Bishop 118

Garrone, Gabriel, Archbishop 38, 84, 91, 149, 168

Gaviola, Mariano, Bishop 86

Gay, Jean, Bishop 102

Gilroy, Norman Cardinal 36

Girgis, Yuhanna, Coptic Orthodox Church 98

Gonçalvez da Costa, Ernesto, Bishop 95

Gracias, Valerian Cardinal 70

Grant, Charles, Bishop 84

Grotti, Giocondo, Bishop 46

Grotoff, Serge, Russian Church Outside of Russia 113, 129

Guana, Emilio, Bishop 38

Hacault, Antonio, Bishop 70

Hallinan, Paul, Archbishop 27

Han Kong-ryel, Peter, Bishop 102

Hannan, Philip M., Bishop 172, 176

Häring, Bernard, C.SS.R. 169

Haubtmann, Peter, Msgr. 41-44

Heenan, John Cardinal 67, 97, 110

Heiser, Basil, O.M., Superior General 36

Hengsbach, Franz, Bishop 48, 63, 74, 132, 151

Herrera y Oria, Angelo Cardinal 109

Hoeffner, Josef, Bishop 74

Holt, Basil, World Convention of the Churches of Christ 92

Houtart, François, Msgr. 79-81

Hromadka, Josef L., Czech Brethren 180

Huenemann, Ruben H., International Congregational Council 136

Hurley, Denis, Archbishop 78

Iakovos, Archbishop, North and South America, Orthodox Ecumenical Patriarchate 179

Indulgences 132-35, 138-42, 144-46, 149, 153-54, 158-59, 180

International Congregational Council 136, 165-66, 178

John XXIII, Pope 7, 13, 62, 93, 97, 127, 152, 157-58, 165, 171, 173, 176, 186

Journet, Charles Cardinal 37, 67, 74

Jubany, Arnau Narciso, Bishop 66-67

Keighley, David Alan, World Methodist Council 43

Kempf, Wilhelm, Bishop 73